swipe

scan

shop

interactive visual merchandising

KATE SCHAEFER

BLOOMSBURY VISUAL ARTS

LONDON • NEW YORK • OXFORD • NEW DELHI • SYDNEY

Contents

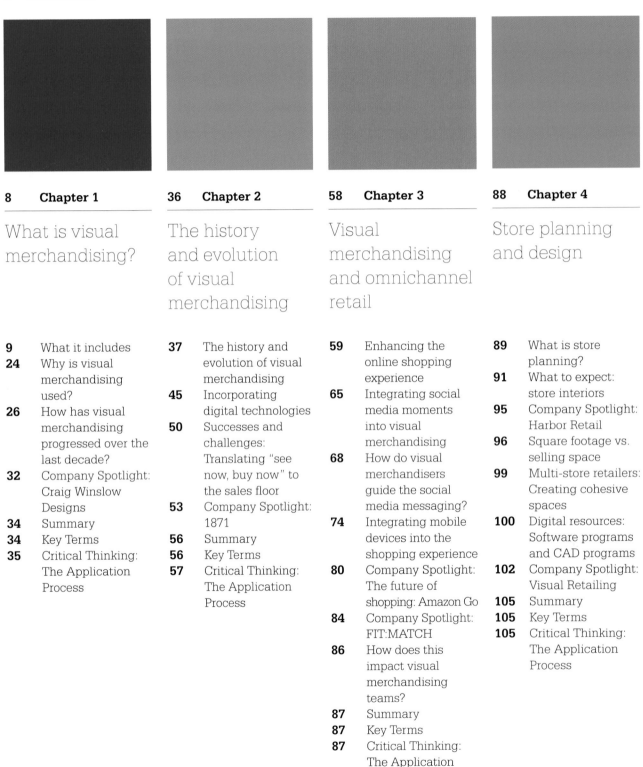

swipe

scan

shop

interactive visual merchandising

BLOOMSBURY VISUAL ARTS
Bloomsbury Publishing Plc
50 Bedford Square, London, WC1B 3DP, UK
1385 Broadway, New York, NY 10018, USA

BLOOMSBURY, BLOOMSBURY VISUAL ARTS and the Diana
logo are trademarks of Bloomsbury Publishing Plc

Cover design by Adriana Brioso
Cover image © Ben Slater/iStock

A catalogue record for this book is available from the British Library.

Library of Congress Cataloging-in-Publication Data
Names: Schaefer, Kate, author.
Title: Swipe, scan, shop : interactive visual merchandising / by Kate Schaefer.
Description: London, UK ; New York, NY, USA : Bloomsbury Visual Arts, 2021.
| Includes bibliographical references and index.
Identifiers: LCCN 2020033100 (print) | LCCN 2020033101 (ebook) |
ISBN 9781350092877 (paperback) | ISBN 9781350092907 (hardback) |
ISBN 9781350092884 (pdf) | ISBN 9781350092860 (epub)
Subjects: LCSH: Merchandising. | Shopping—Technological innovations. |
Display of merchandise.
Classification: LCC HF5415.165 .S33 2021 (print) | LCC HF5415.165 (ebook) |
DDC 659.1/5—dc23
LC record available at https://lccn.loc.gov/2020033100
LC ebook record available at https://lccn.loc.gov/2020033101

ISBN: HB: 978-1-3500-9290-7
PB: 978-1-3500-9287-7
ePDF: 978-1-3500-9288-4
eBook: 978-1-3500-9286-0

Typeset by Lachina Creative, Inc.
Printed and bound in India

To find out more about our authors and books visit
www.bloomsbury.com and sign up for our newsletters.

Introduction

Immersive retail. Branded experiences. Innovative technologies. The brick-and-mortar retail environment is rapidly changing to meet the needs of fickle customers. Retailers are competing with pure play e-commerce sites, omnichannel retailers, and brick-and-mortar retailers for consumer spending in hopes of gaining long-term customer loyalty. The in-store shopping experience is no longer transactional; retailers are looking to build relationships and emotional connections with customers in order to get them back in the store time and time again. Shoppers are looking for quick, convenient, and efficient shopping experiences. Additionally, they are looking for customized experiences based on their own shopping preferences. Is that asking too much?

With the abundance of digital technologies available within the retail industry, customer expectations *can* be met. The use of beacon technologies, facial recognition, touchscreens, and virtual, augmented, and mixed realities in the brick-and-mortar retail environment help retailers create customized, frictionless shopping experiences. However, these experiences are still few and far between in brick-and-mortar shopping.

According to A.T. Kearney's 2019 Consumer Retail Technology Survey, only 33 percent of consumers have experienced any retail technology while shopping. Given the range of opportunities that exist to integrate retail technology in some way throughout the shopping experience, this is a surprisingly low number. Today's consumers are reliant on their mobile devices, so why aren't retailers engaging with customers in this way? What are different ways retailers can integrate digital technologies into the retail environment?

There is a lot of opportunity in the retail industry for the integration of retail technologies, but this integration needs to be relevant; it needs to be well thought out based on target markets and product assortment.

This book provides information and inspiration about how retailers have pushed the envelope to incorporate new technologies throughout brick-and-mortar store environments.

My hope is that retailers and brands embrace innovative retail; that this book reminds retail industry professionals that change is inevitable. Change is necessary in order to stay relevant in the marketplace: **think big**. If at first you don't succeed, try, try again. Change doesn't happen unless we push ourselves to do things differently.

For additional resources on *Swipe, Scan, Shop*, visit this book's Bloomsbury Online Resource at www.bloomsburyonlineresources.com/swipe-scan-shop

0.1
A digital screen used to create a virtual
avatar, center left, is displayed at the
GU Style Studio store, operated by Fast
Retailing Co., in Tokyo, Japan. The GU
Style Studio store is for customers to try
on apparel and place orders online for
later delivery. They can also try out extra
services, such as playing with clothing
combinations on a virtual mannequin and
creating a digital avatar.

1

What is visual merchandising?

Overview

Anything that is visible to a customer within a retail environment is part of visual merchandising; this includes store windows, interior displays, and product presentation, as well as often-overlooked elements such as fitting rooms, signage, and lighting. Visual merchandising is about presenting not only store products, but also brand personality in a favorable way in order to increase sales. It is a form of communication that educates and informs as well as entertains. For this reason, visual merchandising falls within the realm of marketing and the retail environment. This chapter will explain what is included under the visual merchandising umbrella, addressing how digital technologies are integrated into visual merchandising.

1.1
Visual merchandising within a brick-and-mortar retail store is comprised of anything that is visible to a shopper. The new women's accessory department at a Helsinki flagship department store is sleek, clean, and modern, elevating the shopper's expectation of both the merchandise and the retailer's brand aesthetic.

What it includes

Think about the last time you visited a retailer, be it for groceries, electronics, apparel, or accessories. Visual merchandising was all around you, from the exterior signage that you saw as you approached the store, to the product strategically placed that greeted you, and the fixtures that housed all the merchandise. Visual merchandising techniques may have even convinced you to enter a store you had no intention of visiting! Perhaps you were simply window shopping and somehow found yourself inside the store because of compelling store windows or signage. . . you can thank visual merchandising teams for that!

Visual merchandising encompasses everything that is seen in both the store exterior as well as interior. Visual merchandising is used to show brand aesthetic, store concepts, and merchandise at their very best, with the end goal of making a sale; visual merchandising techniques and displays should make the shopping experience more convenient for both the sales associate and the shopper.

For sales associates, effective visual merchandising creates a visual depiction of complete looks, be it on a mannequin or merchandise on a table or a fixture. This makes it easy to grab additional pieces for add-on sales. From a customer perspective, visual merchandising allows shoppers to be more self-sufficient, helping them to envision how products work together. They don't need to rely on employees for styling advice, complementary products, or product information such as pricing, promotions, and even the checkout process. Sales associates can play an important

1.2
How many different types of signage do you see used by Uniqlo?

role in providing customer service and product knowledge, but we've all had shopping experiences where the sales associates were hard to track down, were being pulled in a million different directions, or disinterested in actually doing their job. It is times like these that the suggestive selling tactics from visual merchandising are vital to the selling process. When sales associates are not around and/or interested, let the visual merchandising displays act as the silent salesperson!

As you look around a store, some of the visual merchandising elements you see may include:

- Signage, both retailer and brand-specific
- Lighting
- Fixtures
- Mannequins and forms
- Décor
- Props
- Seating
- Cash wrap
- Interior and exterior displays

A visual merchandiser plays an active role in the selection and placement of these elements in order to create a visually appealing shopping environment that is shoppable and on-brand. Branding must tell a cohesive story for not just the retailer, but the various brands carried within the store as well.

Signage

How might a visual merchandiser tell a cohesive story throughout the retail environment in order to ensure brand cohesion and increase brand loyalty? One way is by using consistent signage. Signage allows retailers to communicate with customers without having to rely on sales associates. When you visit a brick-and-mortar retailer, what types of signage do you see? It is likely that you have seen signage that communicates price, location, and in-store promotions. However, effective signage communicates messaging beyond the written content. Consistent font size, color, and type reinforce brand messages and recognition.

Consistent layout and formatting ensures the intended message is clear and the reader does not spend too much time trying to decipher the message being communicated.

For example, visit your local Nordstrom and look for fixture signage. What you will find is that fixture signage is always the same size, in the same font and color. It is placed on the front right corner of a fixture or front arm on a two-way or three-way. Customers know exactly where to find fixture signage that calls attention to price points, vendor, or trend.

Signage is both retailer and brand specific. What is the difference? Going back to our Nordstrom example, Nordstrom is a specialty retailer that carries an array of brands within their stores. Store signage must adhere to both Nordstrom's standards as well as each individual brand's standards. For example, within Nordstrom's Activewear department, shoppers will find brands such as Nike, Adidas, Champion, and Fila. Departmental signage must include both the Nordstrom corporate signage as well as signage provided by each brand to highlight call-outs such as brand-specific promotions and product knowledge for differentiation within the product category. Shoppers will find Nordstrom's signature silver signage as well as Nike signage that includes their iconic swoosh, or Adidas signage that

1.3
Shoppers at Roots stores are directed to different areas of the store by using signage that plays off the outdoorsy, campy vibe found throughout the store.

features the easily identifiable black and white logo, or Champion and/or Fila's red, white, and blue logo. The branded signage is a clear delineation between these national brands and competing brands housed within the department.

According to Shopify (2018), the five most crucial types of retail signage for a brick-and-mortar store are:

1. **Outdoor signage** gets customers to walk through the doors as it informs passersby as to the name of the store. It sets a tone for both the product offering and brand perception. Have you ever seen a retailer whose store name is not fully illuminated? Or the awning with the store name is ripped, shredded, or otherwise unkempt? These messages communicate that the store, and by default, the merchandise, has not been cared for. Customers don't want to spend their hard-earned money on merchandise they believe is damaged. However, outdoor signage that is well maintained, easy to read, and conveys a polished brand aesthetic communicates to shoppers that the merchandise inside is also well maintained, supporting the story of the brand. Outdoor signage also provides information to passersby, enticing them to enter the store to take advantage of discounts, promotions, and exclusive merchandise.

2. **Informational signage** helps shoppers navigate a store for a more convenient shopping experience. Also referred to as departmental, directional, organizational, or wayfinding signage, informational signage directs customers where to find things within the store. Looking for the elevators? Bathroom? A different department? Informational signage will point shoppers in the right direction. Other examples of informational signage include: customer service, in-store pick ups, departmental signage, ATMs, and exits. Informational signage also reminds shoppers how they can connect with the brand beyond the brick-and-mortar

1.4
Macy's includes both branded signage and persuasive promotional signage to inform and educate shoppers.

location, calling attention to e-commerce sites and social media sites for ongoing communication between the brand and the customer.

3. **Persuasive signage** advertises a promotion or product as a means to increase customer engagement. Persuasive signage is often red sale signage or bold vendor signage to create instantaneous awareness and excitement. You know those "2 for $20" or "Exclusive" signs? Yep, the ones that make you pick up the pace a little as you walk to check out the corresponding product? Those are persuasive signs.

4. **Americans with Disabilities (ADA) Compliant signage** informs customers that the shopping environment is accessible to all customers; customers with disabilities should be able to navigate a store comfortably. This means entrances and exits, fitting rooms, elevators, fixture placement, and signage allow customers with disabilities to navigate the store with ease. ADA compliant signage directs shoppers to elevators, ramps, and bathrooms; these permanent signs should be mounted forty to sixty inches from the

ground (consistent throughout the store) and include Braille and tactile characters.

5. **Mats,** yes, floor mats are signs! Floor mats have the opportunity to feature a logo or brand name for brand reinforcement; they can also be used as informational signage (to direct a customer throughout the store) or promotional signage (to direct a customer to specific product or a sale). For example, North Face used floor mats to direct shoppers to in-store kiosks. As customers walked through the doors to enter the store, they found floor mats with the message "Turn On Explore Mode," which led shoppers to kiosks loaded with digital experiences tied to Earth Day promotions. These digital experiences were designed to encourage customers to be active and explore the outdoors, regardless of where users were located. Users had the opportunity to sign a petition to make Earth Day a national holiday, shop North Face's online store, view their social media sites, and learn about special events and activities. Floor mats can also subtly direct customers from the store entrance to the store interior. As customers enter the store, they often continue walking along the mat until it ends, dropping them at a fixture within the store.

The visual merchandising team is responsible for not only placing signage throughout a store to ensure it is effectively communicating with customers, but they also ensure that signage is visually appealing and on-brand.

Retailers have also been using **digital signage** for added interest, as the messaging is not static; digital signage also provides the ability to tailor messages to different customers as they approach the sign. Digital signage can be messaging projected on a screen, include rotating messaging, and/or use facial recognition to customize messages to different customers. Later in the text we will go into more depth about digital signage.

Lighting

Visual merchandisers source and install lighting throughout the store both for function and aesthetic. All lighting used should be complementary to one another yet effective in creating a shoppable environment. There are many different types of lighting used throughout brick-and-mortar retail; they are often divided into the following categories: ambient, task, accent, and decorative lighting.

Ambient lighting within a retail store is often overhead lighting such as track lighting. It is the main light source in a store and sets the tone for the retail environment, ensuring that the retail environment as a whole is comfortable and shoppers are able to see product throughout the sales floor. For most retailers, ambient lighting ensures that signage, tags, labels, and the merchandise itself is highly visible and easy to read. Most retailers don't want to make their customers work hard to absorb and comprehend their messages. Other retailers, although few and far between, keep ambient lighting dim, creating a sense of mystery and intrigue for shoppers. Abercrombie & Fitch and Hollister, American brands that target the teenage shopper, were once best known for their dimly lit stores. These stores took a different approach to their store environments and created an in-store experience that seemed

1.5
The North Face store captured the attention of shoppers as they walked into the store and were greeted with a mat that read "Turn On Explore Mode." Shoppers were then led to a kiosk where they could explore both the North Face brand as well as various Earth Day promotions.

1.6
The Kate Spade store incorporates different types of lighting throughout the store to illuminate the merchandise as well as enhance the overall store aesthetic.

to be more representative of a club or casino; lighting was dark, windows were covered, and shoppers often found product, signage, tags, and fixtures challenging to see. However, that did not deter the teenage customer from making purchases. They loved that it was not just a retailer, but also a place to hang out with friends. The teens didn't often leave empty-handed, perhaps they unknowingly spent more on the merchandise because they didn't know how much they were paying until they left!

Task lighting, as the name implies, is used to help retailers and shoppers accomplish certain tasks as part of the retail experience. The task could be the checkout process, in which shoppers are signing receipts, or the fitting room, where customers are analyzing fit, color, and product details.

Accent lighting is used to attract shoppers to different parts of the store. Accent lighting is used to draw a customer in (or over) as it focuses on specific parts of the store,

be it merchandise, signage, or a display. The message to shoppers is that the product is noteworthy, as the retailer has gone above and beyond to highlight the product. Accent lighting is often used in store windows to emphasize merchandise, props, mannequins, and signage that is on display, ensuring that customers do not miss the product they are calling attention to.

Last but not least, retailers use **decorative lighting** to increase visual appeal and reinforce the brand image of the retailer. Decorative lighting is less about function and more about visual appeal. Decorative lighting is used to enhance the store aesthetic. For example, a bridal retailer might choose an oversized crystal chandelier as a focal point to create a retail atmosphere that feels luxurious, soft, and feminine. A menswear store might feature lighting with a more urban feel, incorporating light fixtures that are more industrial with black iron frames and Edison

1.7
The Hennes & Mauritz (H&M) store in Madrid uses crystal chandeliers for decorative lighting to create focal points within the store. The chandeliers do not provide much light, but they do enhance the overall store environment. Ambient lighting is used to provide the primary visibility in the store.

light bulbs. These light fixtures are examples of lighting that doesn't illuminate the store or merchandise, but rather reflect the brand aesthetic of the retailer.

Later in the text you will also learn about **customizable lighting**. This trend used by retailers is allowing shoppers the ability to adjust lighting (most often fitting room lighting) to reflect the time of day and/or occasion for which a garment will be worn. This provides shoppers with a more realistic representation of how apparel and accessories will look outside of the retail environment. For example, at Rebecca Minkoff, shoppers can adjust the fitting room lighting according to the time of day the garments will be worn, as evening and daytime looks appear very different at different times of the day and in different lighting.

Regardless of whether the lighting is ambient, task, accent, or decorative lighting, a more sustainable option is the use of LED lighting. LED lighting improves energy efficiency and reduces long-term overhead costs. Although more expensive initially, LEDs not only last longer than the fluorescent light bulbs used in the past, but they are also made of recyclable materials that can be repurposed. Another benefit of utilizing LED lights is that usage can be controlled remotely via an app. Lights can be adjusted based on the different times of day, to spotlight special events, and allows for merchandise to be presented in a more favorable manner by adjusting hues and tones to reduce discoloration.

Fixtures

Fixtures allow retailers to place product on the sales floor, enabling customers to shop in a systematic way. However, fixtures need to be more than simply functional elements on the sales floor; they need to reinforce brand imaging. Fixtures are highly visible, and therefore, must be on-brand to create a cohesive retail environment. Retailers may use temporary or permanent fixtures or a combination of the two.

- **Permanent fixtures** are built into the walls, flooring, or ceiling of the store; the merchandise on the fixtures can change but the fixtures themselves cannot be altered in terms of height, location, or configuration. The height, location, and configuration are permanent.
- **Temporary fixtures** are just that; they can be moved throughout the sales floor depending on product assortment, time of year, and in-store promotions. **Temporary fixtures** have bases or wheels and can be moved throughout the store, relocated throughout the floor, or stored in backrooms to be used on an as-needed basis. Additionally, the height of these fixtures can be raised or lowered depending on the length of the garment; when miniskirts are on trend, the arm of the fixture will be lowered to eye level but when maxi dresses are on trend, the arm of the fixture will increase so that the product is not dragging on the floor.

1.8
Unique fixtures, like using a retro metal swing set, are both functional and eye-catching. It speaks to the unconventional aesthetic of New York City retailer Dover Street Market. Because of the different heights of the swing set, the fixture can be remerchandised to accommodate a variety of garments, ranging from long pants and maxi dresses to shirts, shorts, and skirts.

1.9
The hang bars that line the perimeter of the Prada store on Rodeo Drive are secured into the cement floor; they cannot be relocated or adjusted in any way. They are permanent fixtures in the store.

1.10
Gap stores incorporate a variety of fixtures in order to effectively showcase both the depth and breadth of their inventory. Many of the stainless steel fixtures found in the middle of the sales floor are standard fixtures and can be moved on an as-needed basis. Their wall-mounted fixtures are part of a grid system that allows the retailer to adjust the height of fixtures based on the products featured.

Fixtures can also be standard or custom, freestanding or wall-mounted.

- **Standard fixtures** are manufactured and sold to retailers and businesses; these are often the stainless steel, wood, or plastic fixtures found at majority of retail stores.
- **Custom fixtures,** on the other hand, are designed specifically for a retailer to meet their needs based on brand aesthetic, product offering, and space allocation. They are one-of-a-kind and are only found at the respective retailer.
- **Freestanding fixtures** can be transported throughout a retail space as they are not affixed to the wall or ceiling of a retailer. Freestanding fixtures create flexibility on a sales floor to accommodate different types of merchandise as well as fluctuating inventory levels.
- **Wall-mounted fixtures** are anchored to store walls; oftentimes store shelving is used in the form of wall-mounted shelves. Utilizing shelves allow for large amounts of inventory to be displayed in a relatively small amount of space.

Mannequins and forms

Mannequins and forms bring apparel and accessories to life. We will talk more about mannequins and forms later in the text, but it is important to understand the purpose they serve. Mannequins and forms allow customers to see merchandise on a body, showing product fit and sizing, demonstrating hemlines, necklines, and sleeve length, as well as product details such as pleats and embellishments. Retailers choose mannequins and forms based on their product offering and store aesthetic. Mannequins offer more structure than forms; they are typically made of fiberglass and plastic. **Mannequins** can be full-bodied, headless, or feature just one part of the body (i.e., legs only if you are emphasizing pants, socks, or even shoes). They can be realistic or abstract. **Forms**, on the other hand, are softer to the touch. Their bodies are padded, allowing for pins to be easily stuck into the body for draping and/or display purposes. These soft bodies typically stand atop a cast iron pole and four-wheeled base.

Unlike forms, mannequins are offered in an array of poses. These different poses are used to show personality, movement, and/or product capabilities. For example, mannequins can be standing with their arms crossed or arms on their hips, leaning against one another, or laying horizontally. Retailers that sell activewear, like Nike and Lululemon, use mannequins in active poses such as running or stretching to show the apparel in motion.

Mannequins are now incorporating digital technologies in the form of beacon technologies that inform customers through **push notifications** of product offerings, inventory levels, promotions, and product price points. Push notifications are messages delivered to one's smartphone as pop-up messages delivered via an app; push notifications are a form of one-way communication between the retailer and user. Newly designed mannequins may also include touchscreens to inform, educate, and/or entertain shoppers. This will be addressed in depth in Chapter 6.

1.11 (left)
A window display at Saks Fifth Avenue positions a mannequin and a form side by side.

1.12 (below)
Mannequins that appear to be in motion are ideal for activewear brands. When dressed in athletic apparel, the mannequin poses allow shoppers to see the function of the garments.

Décor and props

Retail environments feature more than just merchandise and fixtures. When looking around many brick-and-mortar stores, you will see various decorative elements that are used to create compelling displays. Props and in-store décor enhance the overall story being told, be it the story of the retailer, season, or promotion. They increase visibility of products, with the end goal of increased sales and profitability.

Social media has played a big role in creating word-of-mouth advertising for retailers and strong visual appeal of in-store displays results in additional sharing via social media. Customer generated content (i.e., shoppers uploading selfies and other lifestyle photos from shopping experiences) have redirected visual merchandisers to create dedicated installations for social media interactions, including backdrops, hashtags, and contests for social media uploads to meet

1.13
Anthropologie stores are as much an art installation as they are a retailer. Art installations throughout the stores are an important part of the retail environment, setting the tone for the type of products customers can expect to find.

the demands and lifestyle of their customers. This has become an important part of the omnichannel retail experience.

Décor and props can be sellable merchandise or simply display items. Sellable merchandise may be brought in from another department, such as candles, books, or stationary from the housewares department, handbags, shoes, or even scarves, jewelry, or hats to tell a more robust or comprehensive story. Props that are simply display items can be purchased new, but oftentimes they are repurposed from previous displays, or purchased second-hand. Remember that visual merchandisers typically have little to no budget to create these compelling displays, so resale shops, dumpster diving, and repurposing old props is often a necessity! When you visit your favorite retailer, have you noticed any decorative props incorporated in displays throughout the store that have taken on a new life? Maybe it has been painted, melted, wrapped in fabric, or deconstructed. . . look closely!

One challenge visual merchandisers face is ensuring that there is a clear delineation between sellable merchandise and decorative elements. It should be clear what products are for sale and what products are simply reinforcing a message for visual appeal.

Seating areas

More and more retailers are choosing *not* to fill their entire sales floor with fixtures and merchandise. Instead, they are incorporating seating areas throughout the floor to give customers not only a physical break, but also a visual break. This visual break gives shoppers a place where their eyes can rest. Shoppers are continually scanning the sales floor, taking in different colors, textures, silhouettes, and embellishments found in merchandise, on mannequins, furniture, signage, both in the physical and the digital space. Shopping can be exhausting!

Seating areas allow for customers to take a break from shopping, sit, and unwind, without having to leave the store. Retailers know all

1.14
Niketown in Chicago added a comfortable and welcoming seating area for guests shopping on Michigan Avenue to relax for a few minutes while still being reminded of the Nike brand through a branded background. Complete with magazines, a coffee table, and greenery, shoppers have the opportunity to unwind from the hustle and bustle of one of the world's busiest shopping districts.

too well that if a customer leaves the store, it is incredibly difficult to get them to come back. It is hard enough to get customers through the door initially, so retailers want to keep them in the store as long as possible! The visual break is a subtle way for customers to breathe a sigh of relief from the retail chaos. These seating areas give customers a chance to check their phones, research products online, or simply get off their feet for a few minutes before they complete their shopping.

Seating areas may also integrate digital components such as smart mirrors, tablets, and free Wi-Fi so customers can still shop and engage with the brand while relaxing for a few moments. These elements help reinforce the brand message and enhance the relationship between the brand and customer. Throughout the text we will discuss various digital components used by retailers to connect, engage, and entertain customers.

Cash wrap

The cash wrap is the last interaction a customer has with a brand when shopping; it is their last point of contact with a retailer. The cash wrap is primarily where customers are rung up, but it is also a point of contact to ask questions, open a credit card, seek additional information, complete a return, etc. The cash wrap used to take up a substantial amount of space on the sales floor; it housed computers, phones, credit card applications, shopping bags, and promotional materials. However, over the years, cash wraps have diminished in size, and even disappeared, in some cases. Cash wraps now might simply be a laptop, tablet, or mobile device. Shoppers are supplying their own bags as part of sustainability efforts, and shoppers seek answers to their questions online, so the products that used to be housed at cash wraps are no longer necessary.

Visual merchandisers work with store planning teams to determine the most appropriate placement for cash wraps as they take up valuable space on the sales floor, yet are important to create an efficient shopping experience for customers. Store planning is discussed in greater detail in Chapter 4. Visual merchandising and store planning teams work together to create a seamless shopping experience for customers, placing the cash wrap in a centrally located area, making it easily accessible, and easily identifiable for customers to ask questions, complete a purchase, or return merchandise, but still in close physical and visual proximity to store entrances and exits for loss prevention efforts. A well-designed and strategically placed cash wrap is a win-win for customers and employees: customer wait times are reduced, customers are engaged and interacting with the brand using digital platforms,

1.15
Permanent cash wraps are disappearing from sales floors as retailers are offering mobile point of sale systems that not only allow customers to checkout, but also obtain information about inventory levels. This radio-frequency identification (RFID) reader operates with a smartphone as employees at Family Mart (Tokyo, Japan) travel throughout the store to provide customer service to shoppers.

and customers are informed of promotions, events, and activities. Employees have clear sightlines throughout the store to assess customers' needs and provide assistance in a timely manner.

Many retailers are eliminating cash wraps all together and utilizing mobile checkouts or frictionless shopping, making the checkout process a seamless experience between the sales team and the customer. This frees up selling space for retailers to use for an array of other purposes. This also leaves a positive impression with customers as the wait time to complete their purchase is greatly reduced, if not completely eliminated.

Interior and exterior displays

Interior and exterior displays are used to attract, inform, and engage shoppers. They reinforce brand messaging for customers and passersby, telling the story of who the retailer is and what they have to offer. The elements used for display purposes create the story for the retailer. For example, based on the use of mannequins, props, signage, and fixtures, what is the aesthetic of the store? Is it clear that the store aesthetic is sophisticated, sporty, or sustainable? Is it geared toward the price-sensitive customer or the trend-conscious customer? Are customers independent shoppers or reliant on the

1.16
Kate Spade is known as a colorful, whimsical brand. Store interiors and exteriors exude this brand personality through not only their product offerings, but through visual displays as well. An arcade game just outside the store entrance at Forum Shops at Caesars Palace invites customers to engage with the brand in an approachable way, subtly directing them inside the store.

1.17
The retail environment of Dover Street Market complements the product offerings. The unique store environment, ranging from wall coverings and fixtures to mannequins and décor, reinforces the overall brand aesthetic.

assistance of sales associates? This type of information can be gleaned from branded signage, the styling of mannequins and forms, and design of fixtures. It is important to remember that although the messaging changes when new product hits the floor, with the launch of promotions, and seasonal changes, the retail story is consistent.

Exterior displays draw in shoppers, both intentional and unintentional customers. Window displays influence 24 percent of purchases; once shoppers have entered the store, they are then further influenced by interior displays.

Window displays and exterior signage inform shoppers about what the retailer stands for in hopes to entice shoppers to venture into the store. Interior displays target shoppers who have already decided to enter the store; these displays are more directed in that the products featured on display are merchandised adjacent to the displays to encourage easy grab-and-go shopping.

Today's shoppers are more informed and educated than ever before. They do their research and visit brick-and-mortar stores simply for transactional purposes; today's customers are not looking to be sold on a product or service. However, displays create visibility of products, which creates awareness. As a result, products that have increased visibility are more likely to be considered in a customer's buying decisions.

What are some tricks to ensure that retail displays are not overlooked?

- Displays should not appear monotonous; vary the height, depth, color, and size of display elements. Hang things from the ceiling, prop them on stands or pedestals, incorporate a mannequin or form to create dimension. Layer front to back, top to bottom.
- Create a focal point; ideally, this is the product you are selling. Create a display around the focal point. This ensures that shoppers know exactly what is for sale and what is being used for visual appeal; they should not have to spend a lot of time trying to figure out what is a decorative prop and what is sellable merchandise.
- Displays are informative; make this information accessible! The products highlighted in the display should be in close proximity to the display itself; remember, the display has (hopefully!) garnered attention for the products,

so strike while it is hot. Customers are interested in the product, so make sure it is easy for them to find. Additionally, if there is something unique about the products featured, include signage! For example, is the product exclusive to your store? Is it comprised of sustainable fabrics? Is it manufactured locally? Is it selling for a discounted price? Create relevancy and awareness based on what is important to your customers.

- Invite your customers to interact with the products. Engage customers in the displays by inviting them to sample product, customize goods, or connect with the brand digitally. Include tablets to direct shoppers to product customization options, **endless aisles**, or social media sites.
- Know that customers have expectations for product price points based on displays. Products that are more expensive should be displayed in an organized, methodical fashion. The more space there is between product, the more expensive customers expect it to be; the more product there is crammed together, the more affordable it appears to be. Sale products are expected to be a bit messier and unorganized; customers looking for a steal enjoy the hunt.
- Invigorate merchandise, both old and new! Move product around so that the sales floor and inventory does not look stale. Repeat customers don't want to see the same products and displays time and time again, so move merchandise around throughout the store. This breathes life into merchandise that has been on the sale floor for a while and also draws attention to new product that just arrived!

The role of visual merchandising has changed over the years and it continues to evolve as store environments adapt to changing consumer behavior and expectations.

Why is visual merchandising used?

Visual merchandising is, surprisingly, not about simply product sell-through. The goal of visual merchandising is to engage and inspire customers. What?!? Not actually sell product? Well, the sales piece is the result of engaged and inspired customers.

Visual merchandising is, also, not just about live merchandise (merchandise that is for sale), but rather the store environment as a whole. Visual merchandising is used to create a compelling retail environment, a retail environment that invites customers to not just shop for product, but also connect with the brand while doing so. This will lead to repeat business. Factors that visual merchandisers must consider include: product offerings, signage, fixtures, branding, lighting, and, of the utmost importance, target market. If the store environment is not appealing to their target market, then shoppers will not venture through the doors into the store. Once shoppers are in the store, merchandising teams strive to create a store environment that makes shoppers feel inspired, engaged, and comfortable; the longer they stay in the store, the more money they will spend. Additionally, in today's social media-driven culture, the longer customers spend in the store, the more likely they are to connect, photograph, and share content with their networks. This is why visual merchandising teams are integral to the story retailers are telling, both in terms of brand aesthetic and product placement.

A shopper's first impression is based on their sense of sight, so creating the overall ambiance is important. The styling of the mannequins, tables, and shelving units must complement interior store elements such as light fixtures, paint colors, and furniture. Signage should be concise and informative. The merchandise should be easily accessible. These elements support one another in cohesive brand messaging.

These merchandising strategies create visually appealing sales floors that also create efficiency for the shopper. Mannequins and decorative displays should be adjacent to product offerings; displays and fixtures include complementary products as a suggestive selling tool. Shoppers don't have the time or desire to seek out merchandise, so ensuring that merchandise is easily accessible through fixtures and displays creates a convenient and efficient shopping experience. Customers are informed of seasonal trends, promotions, and in-store events and activities as a result of visual merchandising. It is all about creating awareness. When products or informational signage is missing, sales suffer. Shoppers don't know what they are missing out on if they can't see it!

1.18
The retail environment at the Tod's store in Paris sets the tone for customer expectations, including product offering, price point, and brand aesthetic.

How has visual merchandising progressed over the last decade?

Visual merchandising used to be the way brands and retailers communicated their in-store messaging to customers; the messaging was developed and created by the brand and pushed out to shoppers through marketing campaigns. However, with the digital space growing and becoming increasingly interactive, brand messaging is now coming from both the retailer and the customer.

Retailers and brands develop messaging that is incorporated for print, digital, and in-store messaging to ensure consistent branding across platforms. Additionally, customers are able to share their experiences,

ask questions, and leave product reviews on retailer websites and social media sites; this affects the overall brand messaging because these messages cannot be controlled by retailers and brands. Oftentimes this brand messaging is found online, but with the integration of the digital and physical shopping environments, the messaging carries over from online to off-line, and vice versa. For example, customers share both positive and negative in-store experiences, ranging from customer service to product assortment, on retailers' social media sites. Retailers have the opportunity to respond, in both public and private forums, to these posts in hopes of assuring their customer base that they are cognizant of and addressing customer needs.

Shoppers in the brick-and-mortar stores are given the opportunity to engage and connect digitally through various touchpoints within the store. Customers are passively exposed to retailer's websites and social media sites; they are also invited to actively engage with the brand by participating in social media moments offered in-store, utilizing hashtags and/or QR codes to learn more about products, or customize merchandise using tablets or kiosks.

Glossier, a beauty and skin-care brand, has become synonymous with in-store design influenced by social media. Glossier stores are filled with Instagrammable moments that inspire shoppers to snap a photo while shopping for their favorite beauty brands. Color, architectural elements, and unique fixtures are all part of the branded experience, which encourages shoppers to connect with the brand through social media engagement

1.19
Topshop uses store windows to call attention to the various ways customers can connect with the brand, both in-store and digitally. Shoppers are reminded of the products and services offered by Topshop as well as ways to connect to seek styling advice and inspiration. Topshop called attention to their Instagram handle for a convenient way for their target market to connect with the brand and see Topshop products on actual customers.

and in-store experiences. This is a logical integration between digital and physical as Glossier began as an e-commerce site in 2014 and launched their first flagship store in New York City in 2017.

As you see, it is not a matter of one or the other, but rather how these two mediums support and complement one another. The online customer is directed to shop in-store and the brick-and-mortar customer is invited to connect virtually, be it through websites, social media sites, or branded apps. Visual merchandising connects the physical and digital presence of a brand by creating a seamless in-store shopping experience; what we see online is easily identifiable in-store to create a sense of familiarity. This has led to the retail sector coining the term "phygital experience."

The **phygital experience** represents the integration of physical and digital commerce. Both the physical (brick-and-mortar) and digital (e-commerce, s-commerce, m-commerce) are incredibly important to retailers. Brick-and-mortar stores allow customers a tactile experience and provide the immediacy and accessibility of products for instant gratification customers; online shopping provides accessibility in terms of increased product offerings as shoppers can access endless aisles at whatever time is most convenient for them.

However, these are no longer siloed experiences; digital and physical shopping experiences no longer act as separate entities. Shopping brick-and-mortar stores integrate components such as touchscreens, QR codes, and beacons, to name a few. Online shopping directs customers to brick-and-mortar stores through buy online, pick up in-store options and in-store returns, among others. As you see, the digital and physical shopping experiences are becoming increasingly blended to provide solutions to the evolving needs and demands of shoppers. The objective of the phygital experience is to customize communication with shoppers by bringing together the online and offline experience.

1.20
In-store shoppers use mobile devices to scan QR codes found on product hangtags in order to access product knowledge. These QR codes allow shoppers to learn more about the products themselves as well as benefits received from making a purchase.

Both retailers and brands, stores and visual merchandisers, have been impacted by the **Internet of Things (IoT)**. The Internet of Things is, in simple terms, a network of connected objects that collect and exchange data through technologies, such as sensors and software programs. What does this mean? First, there is a "thing" (object or device) and secondly, it is connected to the internet. The devices use the internet to send data to other devices; once the data is processed by software systems, alerts or push notifications are sent out or messaging is adjusted as a result of facial recognition.

The integration of IoT in the retail environment allows the customer experience to be more personalized. Messaging found in marketing campaigns is based on customer behavior, creating relevancy to products, services, and benefits received by the customer. And, as a result, customers and retailers are connected in a more meaningful way. Throughout the text you will learn about various IoT elements: Smart Shelves as seen at Amazon Go, beacon technologies, digital signage, and facial recognition, to name a few. These are just a few examples of ways retailers and brands are connecting with customers in a meaningful way.

Visual merchandising is a subtle point of connection. The points of connection are no longer just the personal connection between a sales associate and customer. The connection is made at various touchpoints within a store, from the in-store experience of using a golf simulator to taking a selfie that is featured across social media feeds or customizing a pair of shoes on a tablet to be sent to the customer's home.

Leveraging these existing and new technologies not only act as a portal for customer engagement, but also as a vehicle to enhance the in-store experience.

These digital experiences enable shoppers to play a role in the look and feel of the store by participating in the design of displays. For example, Samsung's 837's store in New York City encourages shoppers to curate the appearance of the store by uploading digital content that is featured throughout the store. Samsung invites shoppers to be part an immersive in-store experience using their very own social media feeds. Called Social Galaxy, the interactive installation features a mirrored tunnel lined with Samsung devices. Users input their Instagram usernames at the entrance and within seconds, the displays pull in images and comments from the input social media accounts, effectively surrounding them with their own social media feeds from all angles. Imagine the different aesthetics created from various accounts and how that impacts the overall store environment. Some Instagram feeds are filled with selfies, others are filled with inspirational quotes, nature, food, or fashion imagery. Inundating a store with these different images dramatically changes the atmosphere.

As you have likely experienced in today's retail environment, the shopping experience has become an active experience between the customer and the brand. It is not just about what customers see, but it is also about what they experience; visual merchandisers must integrate these in-store experiences alongside live merchandise. **Experiential retail**, which we will look at in more depth in Chapter 5, invites customers to be part of the brand through branded experiences, creating an active shopping experience as opposed to a passive shopping experience where the information sharing is one-sided. Branded experiences slow customers down and allow them to experience product usage and benefits. One of the most successful retailers for experiential retail is Apple. Apple products are placed throughout Apple stores in a visually appealing manner; products are turned on, logged on, and fully charged. Customers are able to test out products and product capabilities at their own pace. When they have a question or are ready to make a purchase, sales associates are easily recognizable to answer questions, provide insight, or close the sale by retrieving the product and ringing up the customer on

1.21
In 2004, London retailer Selfridges' exterior windows promoted "The End of the Blind Date" competition. Windows featured contestants interacting with the world's first mobile dating app and preparing to meet their connections. As a result, window displays were continually changing as new contestants ventured into the window to participate in the branded activity.

the spot. The sales floor is dedicated to experiencing the products rather than housing and displaying back stock and additional inventory. This leads us to another movement in visual merchandising, which is eliminating inventory levels on the sales floor; this is addressed throughout the text.

The North Face utilizes experiential retail in an entirely different way in that shoppers are not testing out North Face products, but rather the brand is connecting with shoppers on a personal level as members of the sales team act as "local experts" for their customers. To reinforce their "Never Stop Exploring" messaging, North Face invites customers to explore the local areas in which their stores are located through concierge services, inviting shoppers (primarily tourists) to visit their Guide Center, which is "a place to connect with our associates and share knowledge of activities, travel, the outdoors and Community". Store associates take on the role of tour guide, providing recommendations and insights for shoppers to explore the cities in which they are visiting.

Another dramatic shift in visual merchandising is that the focus is no longer on sellable merchandise, but rather overall retail environment. Retailers are ascribing to the less is more mentality in terms of product offerings on the sales floor (as mentioned above for Apple stores). Retailers are no longer maximizing square footage as it pertains to inventory levels as shoppers find too much product overwhelming and confusing. For example, Origins, a skincare brand focused on

1.22 and 1.23

The North Face store on Chicago's Magnificent Mile invites shoppers in this highly tourist-driven store to use their concierge service to discover the best that Chicago has to offer.

GUIDE CENTER

A Place to Connect with our associates and share knowledge of activities, travel , the outdoors, and Community.

GUIDE CENTER SERVICES:

- MOBILE CHECK OUT.
  - DELIV- SHIP TO HOTEL , HOME OR BUSINESS WITHIN 15 MILES, FREE OF CHARGE.
- ADVENTURE OUTFITTING.
  - SCHEDULE AN INSTORE OUTFITTING EVENT WITH A TNF ASSOCIATE THROUGH EVENTBRITE SCHEDULING.
  - EXPLORE TNF ASSOCIATE PROFILES TO FIND KNOWLEDGE IN YOUR TRAVEL ITINERARY, ACTIVITY OR INTERESTS.
  - RESEARCH YOUR DESTINATION UTILIZING A VARIETY OF TRAVEL APPS.
- LOCAL CONCIERGE:
  - EXPLORE LOCAL COMMUNITY THROUGH OUR ASSOCIATES AND RELEVANT APPS.
- COMMUNITY:
  - OUT OF STORE EVENTS OR PARTNERSHIPS.
- IN STORE EVENTS:
  - LOCAL PARTNERSHIPS
  - NEXT INSTORE PRESENTATIONS
  - PRODUCT LAUNCHES
  - STAY UP TO DATE THROUGH FACEBOOK.

natural ingredients, actually increased in-store sales by 20 to 40 percent when they *decreased* the amount of product on the sales floor. They used the additional square footage to offer in-store experiences for customers to touch, feel, and test the products. In fact, retailers are now offering entire stores with no product to sell. Seems crazy, right? A store with no merchandise? This represents the shifting dynamics in shopping behaviors.

Nordstrom has opened a smattering of Nordstrom Local stores; these stores are much smaller in size and are missing one very important element in the retail experience: sellable product! The goal is that these smaller, experiential spaces allow Nordstrom customers to develop stronger relationships with sales associates. Nordstrom Local stores are a fraction of the size of Nordstrom full-line and Nordstrom Rack stores (3,000 square feet as opposed to 140,000 square feet) and emphasize customer service rather than selling. The stores have fitting rooms, an on-site tailor and seamstress, nail salon, and bar. Although there is no inventory to purchase on site, Nordstrom Local stores will include some apparel and accessory items for shoppers to try on. Additionally, these smaller stores will also allow customer returns from other retailers, such as Macy's and Kohl's, regardless of whether or not Nordstrom is selling the same product.

How does a retail store with no inventory actually work? Upon entering the store, stylists are on hand to assist shoppers digitally to create a personalized wardrobe; customers can order merchandise online to be delivered to the store that same day rather than having to wait for items to be shipped to their home. Or, for an even faster delivery option, the stylists can visit the nearest traditional Nordstrom locations to retrieve the items, returning to the Nordstrom Local store for customers to try on. If shoppers want to wait for the clothing to arrive, they can have a drink or visit the nail salon for a manicure while their stylist gathers their order. Once the requested items arrive at the Nordstrom Local location, tailors and seamstresses are available on-site to make any necessary alterations.

Online Nordstrom shoppers are encouraged to ship online orders to Nordstrom Local stores, if available in their area. Upon pick up, customers can conveniently try on their orders; a seamstress is readily available to provide expert knowledge of fit and alterations or, if the purchase is not what the customer expected, they can complete their merchandise return immediately. The footprint of the store is more manageable than full-line stores and the focus on customer service makes the in-store pick up experience more conducive to relationship building between the customer and the retailer.

1.24
Nordstrom Local concept store in Manhattan (NYC) will accept merchandise returns from rivals like Macy's Inc. and Kohl's Corp. in the new small-format locations, regardless of whether Nordstrom carries the same item.

Company Spotlight: Craig Winslow Designs

Named illumifeet, Winslow used interactive projection mapping and sensing technology to inform, educate, inspire and entertain passersby.

Craig Winslow runs a creative design lab that focuses on the integration of the physical and digital worlds; his work infuses graphic design, 3D art, and new, old, and emerging technologies. What does this mean for the retail environment? Installations, exhibits, and collaborations that push the boundaries. For example, floating shoes? Check! Projection displays? Check! Sensory experiences? Check, check, check!

Craig Winslow Designs' client list spans various industries, including the likes of Nike, Coca-Cola, Portland Trail Blazers, and Princeton University. A particularly noteworthy installation from Craig Winslow Designs is a set of collaborative windows Winslow created for sneaker company Bucketfeet's New York City pop-up shops. (Bucketfeet is an artist-driven sneaker company that sells handmade-to-order shoes.) Winslow's first window for Bucketfeet was designed for the brand's six-week residency at Treasure & Bond. (Now closed, Treasure &

Bond was a Nordstrom-owned temporary retail operation in the SoHo neighborhood in New York City.) The second window was created for a Bucketfeet-owned pop-up shop in New York City, just down the street from the Treasure & Bond storefront. The windows became must-see destinations in New York's SoHo neighborhood as the interactive displays "turned on" when the store closed, generating excitement and awareness of Bucketfeet product 24 hours a day, 7 days a week.

Named illumifeet, Winslow used interactive projection mapping and sensing technology to inform, educate, inspire, and entertain passersby. The focus of the window was a pair of white canvas sneakers discreetly hanging from the store ceiling using fishing wire. The sneakers appeared to be floating in the air above a feature table that housed a white cube surrounded by an array of Bucketfeet sneakers displaying varying designs sold by the company.

1.25–1.29
Projection mapping was used to create an active window, showing the various designs of the sneakers available for purchase.

As shoppers approached the window display, sensing technology was activated and the projection mapping began. Bucketfeet's new designs were projected onto the blank shoe, allowing viewers to see exactly what the actual printed shoe looks like. As the designs were projected onto the shoe, information about the artist was projected onto the cube below. As long as shoppers continued watching the display, the images rotated through. Every few seconds a new design was projected onto the sneaker with corresponding artist messaging on the cube, giving viewers an opportunity to see a range of product offerings in a short amount of time. As soon as the viewer walked away from the window, both the shoes and the cube returned to solid white.

When Bucketfeet opened a second pop-up shop the following year, they once again tapped Winslow to design the window. Building off of the Treasure & Bond window, Bucketfeet's second pop-up shop window featured another round of projection mapping, but on a larger scale. Rather than dangle the sneakers from the ceiling, the white canvas sneakers appeared to be balancing atop a jagged peak. The larger foundation allowed for a greater surface area for the projection mapping to display both the artwork and artist information.

The projection mapping used in these windows brought information about the different Bucketfeet designs directly the customers; customers did not have to seek it out by talking to a sales associate, shopping the collections, or clicking through online. It was an effortless process for customers to learn about Bucketfeet's shoe assortment as information was pushed to these shoppers rather than requiring customers to seek out new designs themselves.

Another collaborative partner Winslow worked with was Nike during the launch of Riccardo Tisci's second collaboration with Nike (NikeLab x RT). The collection was inspired by the jungles of Rio de Janeiro, so Winslow used motion patterns to bring the print designs of Riccardo Tisci to life. Winslow digitized the print designs by projecting Tisci's floral designs as they grew and became intertwined with one another. These animations captivated viewers as they watched and waited to see how the image evolved. Once the screen was fully engulfed in flora, the Nike x RT logo was displayed. The projected animations were consistent with the floral designs included in NikeLab x RT collection, increasing awareness of limited edition apparel. Winslow's animations were projected throughout NYC and Rio de Janeiro in various locations as interior and exterior installations as well as at Nike retail stores worldwide.

Summary

Visual merchandising is all encompassing of the retail environment; it includes anything and everything that visible to shoppers. As buyer behavior shifts, the retail environment must adapt. This includes brick-and-mortar stores, integration of new technologies, and the in-store experience.

Because of the depth and breadth of digital capabilities, the brick-and-mortar retail environment is no longer visible to only in-store shoppers; it is now visible and accessible to a global audience with the push of a button. Retailers are working to have more control over the digital content by creating dedicated in-store experiences to connect with and share virtually.

As you continue reading, you will see that this topic is the basis of much of the chapter readings that are forthcoming in the text. You will learn how retailers are using digital technologies throughout the brick-and-mortar shopping experience, both to control the messaging and to engage their customer. However, keep in mind this is not an exhaustive list as the capabilities of digital technologies are changing faster than ever.

KEY TERMS

Accent lighting
ADA Compliant signage
Ambient lighting
Customizable lighting
Decorative lighting
Endless aisles
Experiential retail
Informational signage
Internet of Things (IoT)
Outdoor signage
Persuasive signage
Phygital experience
Task lighting
Visual merchandising

CRITICAL THINKING: THE APPLICATION PROCESS

After completing the chapter readings, reflect on the information and experiences shared. Apply what you learned to future retail experiences:

1. Finding inspiration from Dover Street Market's retro swing set as a fixture, what are two unexpected fixtures that could be incorporated into a store? What store(s) do you recommend for these fixtures?

2. As retailers choose to add seating areas to their sales floors, what might be included in the seating area in order to further connect with shoppers?

3. Imagine you work for a large retailer. The departmental budget allows for you to make one purchase of a decorative prop that has the potential to be repurposed throughout various departments. What will you purchase? Explain at least three different ways you plan on repurposing it for different departments.

4. As buyer behavior changes, what other retail components might fall under the purview of visual merchandisers?

5. Why is the Internet of Things important for visual merchandising teams?

2

The history and evolution of visual merchandising

Overview

In order to understand the 'why' of visual merchandising, it is important to know how and when it all began. Chapter 2 will look at the history of visual merchandising over the past century, addressing how it is has evolved from one decade to the next. Visual merchandising is no longer simply displaying products; it now includes the immersion of digital technologies and sensory merchandising. It is important for retailers to understand how to create displays that appeal to shoppers' senses.

2.1
At the Saks Fifth Avenue NYC Flagship store, the unveiling of six Frozen 2 themed windows was a multi-channel experience as it also included a musical performance by Idina Menzel (the voice of Elsa), a character meet-and-greet for children, as well as live streaming of the event on both Saks. com/Holiday and Disney. com.

The history and evolution of visual merchandising

At the start of retailing, the store environment was less than desirable. Customers did not peruse and/or window-shop. Customers visited stores to make intentional purchases; they would speak with the store owners about their needs and the store owner would disappear into the back room and reappear with the product for purchase. Shoppers were at the mercy of store owners; they had no idea about product assortment, inventory levels, complementary products, or comparable products. However, at the end of the eighteenth century, store owners began offering a sensory experience to customers through visual display.

The first known examples of visual merchandising were found in the 1800s when retailers began displaying merchandise in store windows or on exterior tables to lure customers in; retailers carefully selected their best merchandise and arranged it in a highly visible location, easily accessible to passersby. It became apparent that this was effective as customers entered the store asking for the products seen on display. It didn't matter what the product was, as long as it was visually appealing; this created a need for customers. Butchers chose the best cuts of meat, grocers put the most vibrant and largest produce on the top of the stack, and florists placed the freshest cut stems in the most prominent spot in their window. Sales quickly increased, which store owners attributed to the exterior product displays. Shopping was no longer driven by customer need, but rather driven by desire, which oftentimes was an impulse purchase derived from displays.

This thoughtful product placement then trickled to store interiors, resulting in in-store visual merchandising displays. If exterior displays enticed customers to come in the

2.2
A grocer stands in front of his well-stocked display outside his store.

store to make a purchase, then surely interior displays would do the same! And they did. . . these displays encouraged the consumers to remain in the store for more than destination shopping. Customers were purchasing products as a result of suggestive selling or choosing products that were made readily available to them through displays. The result was a convenient and enjoyable shopping experience, creating loyal customers who, because of their positive retail experience, opted to return to the same store time and time again. This created a shift in consumer behavior; previously, customers visited a store and spoke with the store owner about a specific item they were looking to purchase. However, once displays were used to introduce customers to an array of products, retail became more of a self-service experience and encouraged customers to browse available products.

Retailers realized that the visual merchandising displays created product relevancy as it pertained to customer lifestyle; the displays acted as suggestive selling tools for customers. Not only were customers exposed to an array of products, but the displays also enabled them to visualize how these products fit into their lifestyle. Shoppers were already sold on an item before asking for help from store owners; this resulted in less selling (information sharing, product knowledge, etc.) and more transactional purchases. Shoppers relied on store owners to simply ring them up to complete the sale.

Visual merchandising displays continued to be a significant tool for retailers into the mid-1800s, to attract and entice consumers. These techniques not only showcased the most attractive products, but also featured available merchandise, which allowed store owners to sell through their inventory much faster. Visual displays allowed retailers to subtly push products that were available in abundance by creating awareness of product availability.

In the 1840s, the Industrial Revolution brought about new technologies that afforded store owners new opportunities: lighting as well as production of larger glass windows. Large glass windows created store windows as we know them today; store owners were able to create dramatic displays that rivaled theatrical productions. Merchandise featured in store windows allowed customers to be better informed of the array of products carried in-store; shoppers were also intrigued at what they might find, as previously customers shopped with specific products in mind rather than allowing the retailer to inform them of product offerings. These windows were a way to draw customers in through entertainment and then get them to come back during store hours because of the vast array of merchandise that had been featured in the window.

Another turning point in the retail industry came in 1852 when Le Bon Marche opened its

2.3
Department store in Paris Le Bon Marche (founded in 1852 by Aristide Boucicaut, 1810–1877), here c. 1900.

doors in Paris; Le Bon Marche is recognized as the first department store in the world. Compared to specialty stores, which was all that existed before Le Bon Marche opened its doors, department stores are much larger in size and offered an array of merchandise for shoppers. Store windows became increasingly important as customers were able to gather information about product offerings through these visual displays. Window displays were used to inform passersby of the vast array of products available for purchase both through visual displays as well as through window signage. Unfortunately, displays were visible only during store hours when store lights were fully illuminated.

In 1870, what we know today as a mannequin was introduced to retail displays. Made of wax with false teeth, glass eyes, and real hair, mannequins were designed as realistic interpretations of people wearing clothing, and shoppers responded favorably. They were drawn to these displays and retailers found that the use of mannequins influenced overall store sales. One historian stated, "Such was the allure of the then-wax figures that window-shopping quickly became a form of entertainment; millions came to stare at a make-believe world frozen in place" (Mannequin Madness).

The early 1900s brought about two important changes. In 1909, the department store Selfridges began to leave window lights on overnight, allowing customers to browse potential purchases regardless of store hours. Thus the idea of window-shopping was born, making store merchandise visible to shoppers whether or not the retailer was open for business. Another important change in window display was Macy's introduction of animatronic windows. The mechanical holiday displays, which didn't (and still don't) feature sellable merchandise, are simply a form of entertainment. These windows draw in millions of visitors to see the themed displays. Since their inception, the animatronic windows have acted as a tourist attraction to Macy's flagship stores across the country.

The hope is that window shoppers will stop in to purchase either wants or needs; perhaps a gift during the holiday gift-giving season or a pair of gloves, scarf, or hat to protect shoppers from the winter elements as they view the windows.

During the Great Depression of the 1930s, window displays were used as a form of escapism. While consumers were not out shopping for anything except necessities, they were window-shopping. Exterior displays acted as a distraction from the stresses of their everyday lives, as people were struggling to put food on the table and clothes on their backs. Mannequins represented fantastical lifestyles that gave shoppers hope for the future. These displays represented optimism.

The 1960s introduced the use of mannequins as a means to address social trends in window displays. When used as part of store window displays, social trends, or behavior and/or activities that are participated in by society as a whole, created a sense of community between retailers and customers.

Mary Quant, a British fashion designer, changed the way window displays were

2.4
Mary Quant, standing inside the window of her fashion shop Bazaar, alongside mannequins wearing her designs.

used as she used her store windows to show her seasonal collections on mannequins as well as create awareness of social trends in the marketplace. Windows were used for informational purposes, both for merchandise offerings and as a point of connection between societal trends and merchandise offerings. The use of mannequins allowed shoppers to see her collections from the street and better understand fit and styling, giving shoppers an idea of how they would look in Quant's designs. The styling was also used to inform shoppers of developing social trends (at that time, youthfulness and unconventionality in fashion), inviting them to connect with like-minded customers through dress.

During the 1970s and 1980s, store windows reflected societal trends in terms of what was happening in shoppers' daily lives. The design, styling, and interaction between mannequins in store windows was a depiction of the realities in customers' day-to-day lives. Mannequins became more realistic, including different ethnicities, body shapes and facial expressions.

In the 1990s, window and in-store displays became part of marketing departments; large retailers and designers spent elaborate marketing budgets to feature product promotion in their windows. Mannequins were replaced with oversized images of supermodels wearing store products, creating aspirational displays. Shoppers looked to connect with and/ or emulate the lifestyle of the supermodels seen in the windows, catalogs, and in-store graphics. Shoppers lost interest in the 'no name' mannequins they had previously turned to in store windows for inspiration, making it incredibly difficult for smaller retailers and independent retailers to compete.

As window displays became aspirational, consumers were no longer seeking store displays that reflected their lifestyle. Instead, customers sought out store displays that were inspiring and entertaining. These windows became a way to create a type of fantasyland or dreamland, giving the viewer an opportunity to escape reality. Mannequins were used to enhance these fantasies and adhered to societal expectations and standards for beauty: tall and slender with tiny waists. Mannequins were modeled after celebrities and movie stars as opposed to the everyday consumer. Rootstein mannequins, one of the leading manufacturers of realistic mannequins, were often used to create aspirational window installations. Still today, Rootstein designs mannequins that are replicas of models, celebrities, and socialites such as Beyoncé, Cher, and Joan Collins.

2.5
Realistic mannequin manufacturer Rootstein created a Beyoncé collection. This is just one example of mannequins that are designed based on celebrities. Rootstein Beyoncé mannequins wear The Blonds dresses during the Rootstein Presents: Phillipe Blond—"The Blonds Collection—A Retrospective."

However, aspirational displays were short-lived. In the late 1990s, people began to feel disconnected with the retail environment. Displays were unrealistic as consumers could not relate to the look and lifestyle of models, celebrities, and socialites featured in store windows. The aspirational windows felt unattainable. As a result, visual merchandising displays shifted; displays were created to depict the lifestyle of the retailer's target market, making it much more relatable and/or attainable for customers. Not only did store windows reflect these shifts, but mannequins did as well. Realistic mannequins became more representative of mainstream consumers and a representation of one's lifestyle. Realistic mannequins were designed in all different shapes and sizes to reflect consumers of varying sizes, shapes, and ages, including maternity, petite, and plus size. Realistic mannequins that represented the retailer's target market were used to show merchandise on the body. These apparel and accessory displays showed customers complete looks, giving shoppers an idea of how apparel and accessory items would look from head to toe on a body that more closely resembled theirs.

Retailers selling furniture and other housewares displayed products in a way that allowed shoppers to envision how products would look in their own homes. Dining room tables were set with placemats, silverware, plates, and napkins; couches were merchandised with throw pillows, blankets, and coffee tables. Crate and Barrel and Pottery Barn, American housewares retailers, are well known for their aspirational yet relatable lifestyle displays. Customers who are shopping for dining room tables, for example, often add items such as tablecloths, napkins, flatware, and serving pieces to their purchase to recreate the look of the in-store display at their own home.

2.6
Mannequins wait to be painted at the Goldsmith Factory in New York City. To keep up with ever-changing fashion trends, Goldsmith sculptors, molders, and stylists produce not only male and female mannequins but also children, pregnant women, and even animals. Goldsmith has been supplying mannequins to the world's leading fashion retailers since 1927.

These interior and exterior displays gave customers an idea of how the merchandise would fit into their lifestyle; shoppers could see themselves in the displays. As customers envisioned themselves using the products featured in the display, sales increased and units sold per transaction skyrocketed.

When the use of mannequins in windows became stale and redundant, marketing departments began replacing window mannequins with oversized graphics and images of models and celebrities as brand spokespeople. The use of models and celebrities generated excitement and buzz, and became a new way to attract customers. As models and celebrities splashed the pages of magazines and billboards in branded advertisements, these same images were then used as oversized graphics in windows. It became a different type of lifestyle image, representing merchandise in an aspirational yet attainable way. The images depicted product being used in various environments,

many which likely could not be effectively recreated in a window display.

Eventually, the oversized graphic images came alive through television screens as digital technologies evolved. Runway shows and ad campaigns were no longer static. Shoppers were drawn in as they felt like they had front row seats to highly sought-after runway shows; they were also able to see product in motion on models as they strut the runways and sashayed through photo shoots. Product was brought to life and customers bought into this as "their reality."

At the turn of the century in 2000, most people had access to the internet and this became an important part of customers' daily lives. The internet went from a research-based platform to a platform for information gathering, buying, and selling. Shoppers had access to their favorite stores 24 hours a day; they were not limited to stores based on geographic location and/or hours of operation. It was a slow process for consumers to

2.7
Pottery Barn hosted a Nathan Turner book launch. A table place setting designed by Turner is highlighted at the Pottery Barn store as guests sipped on champagne and sampled small plates. Not only were guests able to get their books signed, but they also shopped the lifestyle products carried at Pottery Barn.

adapt to the e-commerce model, as security concerns arose, as did consumers' desire (or lack thereof) to wait for their orders to arrive. However, when the convenience of online shopping took hold, shoppers did not look back. Visual merchandisers were challenged to come up with new ways to get shoppers into brick-and-mortar stores to make a purchase, rather than shopping online from the comfort of their homes.

Visual merchandising teams began integrating eye-catching, decorative elements such as props, live flora, and special events into the in-store shopping experience to create an ambiance and lifestyle environment that customers could relate to or aspire to; this got customers off their couches and into stores. The brick-and-mortar shopping experience felt special and luxurious, providing customers tiny moments to escape from their daily routines.

Once in-store, sales associates were armed with product knowledge, credit card offers, loyalty rewards, and "gift with purchase" rewards for customers. These incentivized customers to make in-store purchases rather than place online orders.

However, with the economic downturn in 2008, customers were not shopping; retailers were struggling. Many closed their doors; for those that did not, budgets were slashed. Visual merchandising budgets were the first to go. The shopping experience that customers had become accustomed to changed yet again as retailers utilized fewer props and specialty items in displays because of budget constraints. Visual merchandisers still tried to meet customer needs and began repurposing props and decorative items. A chair, table, or decorative trunk got painted, recovered, or simply relocated within a store as a way to breathe new life into it. Retailers continually ran sales and promotions in hopes of enticing shoppers to visit the store. As the economy slowly improved, shoppers became accustomed to continual sales and promotional offerings, which greatly impacted retailers' merchandising strategies. Visual merchandisers worked to integrate promotional signage throughout the store

without inundating customers with written messaging, ensuring the focus was always on the product itself. Merchandising teams also worked hard to re-educate customers on the value of full price products as customers were accustomed to consistent sales and they were also comparison shopping online to find lower prices. Visual merchandisers used specialty fixtures, signage, and novelty props to attract attention and create a sense of urgency to purchase new release, special order, and on-trend merchandise at full price. Brick-and-mortar retailers realized this was a point of differentiation in terms of setting themselves apart from e-tailers, as the two shopping channels operated independently of one another.

In 2018, brand storytelling became a buzzword; retailers and visual merchandising teams began integrating the online and digital shopping experience into one through brand storytelling. **Brand storytelling** means that retailers are using shopping platforms to share the brand's story with customers, from the history to behind-the-scenes activities and

2.8
Athleta, a fitness and lifestyle brand under Gap Inc., seeks to inspire active and confident women and girls through their product offerings as well as community events. They host in-store events and excursions that coincide with the company's mission.

2.9
The Lego Store created a photo backdrop out of Legos to attract shoppers to the store. Retailers are now incorporating opportunities for shoppers to create lasting memories with the brand by creating opportunities for shoppers to jump in and be part of the display, snap a photo, and share it with their networks. This creates an emotional connection with brand, but also increases brand awareness through the sharing of user generated content on social media platforms.

social interactions. The goals of retail past (maximizing selling space, inventory levels, and merchandising fixtures on the sales floor) took a backseat to brand storytelling. Sales floors utilized imagery, fonts, colors, textures, and historic elements as well as events and activities to tell their branded stories. Websites began including historical information, links to social media sites, and community involvement recommendations alongside e-commerce shopping for cohesive branding. These all reinforce the brand's storytelling as customers are actively involved and engaged in the retail experience, from learning about

the brand's history to customizing product and connecting via social media.

Along with brand storytelling, experiential retail became an expectation as retailers introduced ways for customers to test out products before making a purchase, customize products, or share purchases and/or shopping experiences with family and friends via social media. According to market research firm NPD's report on experiential retail, "The idea is that a retailer offers consumers a chance to buy an experience rather than just an object or service. . . the consumer buys a memory." Sales floors integrate treadmills and rock-climbing walls for customers to test active wear apparel and accessories; cooking classes give shoppers the opportunity to test utensils and ingredients; athletic retailers offer workout classes; brick-and-mortar retailers act as a meeting spot for field trips and group adventures. As priorities shift, consumers take more pride in doing "things"; (especially "things" that can be shared on social media!) than owning "things."

Visual merchandising, in this way, is used as a silent salesperson; it provides an opportunity for brands and retailers to suggest, inspire, and inform customers throughout their shopping excursions. Displays are used to suggest complementary products and styling recommendations in addition to connecting with and inspiring customers. Customers learn not only about seasonal trends, designers, and product availability, but also community events and brand history. As seasons change, holidays near, and events transpire, displays are used to engage and inform customers. For example, in the United States, as the Kentucky Derby approaches, visual merchandisers nationwide install displays that encourage shoppers to don a Derby-worthy hat, a southern dress, and/or preppy suit to celebrate Derby festivities, even if you are nowhere near Churchill Downs to attend the world-renowned horse race.

Incorporating digital technologies

When retailers stopped trying to compete with the online shopping experience and took the "if you can't beat 'em, join 'em" mentality, consumers responded favorably; thus, omnichannel retail was born. **Omnichannel retail** offers the ability for retailers to create a seamless shopping experience across a variety of shopping channels, bringing the online shopper into the store and directing the brick-and-mortar shopper to digital platforms such as e-commerce and social commerce. (**Social commerce**, or s-commerce, is the newest form of e-commerce. It provides shoppers the ability to make a purchase directly through social media sites.) Through omnichannel retail, customers are integrating various platforms and mediums in which to connect brands and retailers to their daily routine.

It is important to note the difference between omnichannel retail and multi-channel retail. **Multi-channel retail** is the availability to shop via different channels. Multi-channel retail provides various channels for customers to shop, but these channels are not integrated with one another. Prior to the dominance of e-commerce, shoppers found themselves making purchases via catalogues, television, and in-store. However, these shopping outlets were disconnected from one another. The rise of online shopping, done via app, e-commerce, s-commerce, and **conversational commerce**, allows brands, retailers, and customers to communicate with one another across the various platforms. Items placed in a customer's virtual shopping cart on the app will also show up in their shopping cart on the

2.10 and 2.11
The first floor of the American Girl store uses iPads to bring the stories to life for each of the original American Girl dolls. Shoppers are invited to click through the iPad to learn about the lifestyle and time period for the doll. Photo credit: K. Schaefer

e-commerce site. Taken one step further, the digital shopping experience is now intertwined with brick-and-mortar shopping. Shoppers can now access virtual shopping carts through screens found within brick-and-mortar stores. Visual merchandisers are integrating the online shopping experience into the brick-and-mortar store, allocating valuable selling space to kiosks, tablets, and social media activities as part of their omnichannel retail experience, allowing shoppers to complete their online shopping in-store.

Retailers are incorporating digital technologies in various ways throughout brick-and-mortar stores. These evolving technologies allow shoppers to be better informed of the brand's history, retail and design processes, branded innovations, and product usage. The integration of digital technologies in brick-and-mortar stores creates a reason for customers to visit the physical storefront rather than simply shopping online.

Digital screens

The American Girl store has effectively incorporated various forms of digital screens throughout their brick-and-mortar stores in order to educate, entertain, and engage shoppers and, as a result, capture sales. These technologies target different shoppers within their stores, reminding shoppers of the benefit to shopping in-store rather than making a transactional purchase online.

- iPads: As customers enter the store, the first floor utilizes iPads to help tell the stories of the original American Girl dolls. Each original American Girl doll has a dedicated vignette that features memorabilia from the time period in which they were born. To activate this memorabilia, iPads are placed adjacent to display vignettes for each doll, inviting shoppers to learn more about not only the doll, but also the time period in which she

2.12
A digital screen between the first and second floors of the American Girl store in Chicago depicts American Girl dolls in the arms of their owners to show shoppers how the dolls fit into one's lifestyle. The images pull on the heartstrings of shoppers as they see joyful doll owners embracing their American Girl doll, completely outfitted in American Girl apparel and accessories.

lived. Information includes a brief history lesson about the era, social issues that were apparent during the time period, music that was popular, and sports highlights.

- iPads are also used in the customization station, allowing shoppers to create a one-of-a-kind doll. (More information on the customization station is included in Chapter 5, Store interiors.)
- Digital screens: Oversized screens welcome shoppers to the store. Brick-and-mortar stores feature an oversized screen with rotating lifestyle images of American Girl dolls with their owners.

At the Under Armour Brand House, shoppers can't help but notice the vignette and digital signage introducing the brand's newest textile innovation: UA RUSH, a mineral-infused fabric that is scientifically proven to boost athletes' energy while working out. Under Armour provides a lot of information about the fabric itself, the improved performance of the athlete, and re-emitted energy; it is a lot of information to convey through signage, so instead, Under Armour utilized digital screens for condensed, easy to understand rotating messaging. The digital screens inspire shoppers, bringing out the athlete in everyone; they provide a lot of information about the attributes and benefits of the UA RUSH products, allowing readers to take in the information as quickly or slowly as needed. The vignette and screens work simultaneously to excite and inform shoppers about garments for "enhanced performance that is scientifically tested, athlete proven" (underarmour.com). The mineral-infused shirts, offered in a variety of colors, are strategically housed on shelves adjacent to the screen for an easy pick up; the backdrop on the wall behind the vignette is an oversized image of basketball great Steph Curry wearing the mineral-infused shirt. The subtle message? If it is good enough for Steph Curry, it is good enough for you!

2.13 and 2.14
A smaller-scale example of digital signage on the retail sales floor. Digital signage is used to educate shoppers at the Under Armour Brand House on technologically enhanced fabrics that increase an athlete's performance on the field or court.

The connected fitting room

As you know, visual merchandising includes anything and everything that is visible to customers; this means not only the sales floor, but the fitting rooms as well.

Connected fitting rooms, also referred to as smart fitting rooms, are being utilized to create more convenient shopping experiences as customers try on merchandise. Connected fitting rooms connect shoppers to the retail environment, allowing customers to not only communicate wants and needs to store associates, but also customize their fitting room experience. **Smart mirrors** are often an integral part of the connected fitting room. Where customers would typically look into a mirror to gauge fit and styling of garments, smart mirrors integrate a mirrored finish with a touchscreen as a form of communication. Smart mirrors have varying capabilities.

At Rebecca Minkoff stores, shoppers spend more time in the fitting rooms because of the smart capabilities offered. Shoppers can order a drink to be delivered to the fitting room, request additional products (be it a different size or complementary product) to be brought to the fitting room, adjust lighting or create their own personal shopping profile all through a touchscreen mirror in the fitting room. Because the store uses **RFID technology**, items brought into the fitting room are recognized and displayed on the fitting room screen; complementary products are recommended to complete each look. Radio frequency identification is technology that relies on radio frequency waves to emit signals to RFID readers. These signals are read and processed by a software system that provides real-time updates to track stock, manage inventory levels, and access customer order history, among other things. The interactive touchpoints connect the shopper to the brand, streamline the shopping experience, and reinforce the Rebecca Minkoff brand messaging. These services enhance the shopping experience during one of the final stages of the customer's shopping excursion, resulting in improved perceptions of both the retailer and product offerings.

Van Heusen's smart mirror, or Virtual Trial mirror, allows customers to virtually try garments on without having to step foot into a fitting room. Shoppers scan the item's barcode and wait for the garments to be virtually projected onto their reflection. For customers who opt for a fitting room experience, the interactive mirrors snap photos of different outfits, allowing the shopper to compare each look side-by-side to ease the decision-making process.

Targeting an entirely different customer, Abercrombie & Fitch (A&F) also improved the fitting room experience by creating fitting room suites to attract the teenage shopper. The fitting room suites aim to create a fun shopping experience in which groups can go in and try clothes on at the same time in walled-off parts of the same space, allowing for a show-and-tell type experience. The social shopping experience also encourages shoppers to take photos of one another in A&F's newest merchandise and share it with their social media networks. The fitting room suites also allow customers to adjust the fitting room lighting, charge their phones, or listen to their playlists while shopping with their friends.

2.15
The connected fitting room at Rebecca Minkoff's SoHo store allows customers to continue shopping the brand's inventory without leaving the fitting room. It also makes product recommendations, allows customers to adjust lighting, and complete the checkout process without the help of sales associates.

While most smart mirrors are used to connect shoppers with sellable product and sales teams, Canadian-based athleticwear retailer Lululemon uses smart mirrors as a form of community building. In their Manhattan and Vancouver flagship stores, smart mirrors are placed in the middle of the sales floor, making them easily accessible to shoppers so they can be educated about happenings in the local community, including special events, where to workout, and lifestyle recommendations.

These are just a few examples of how brick-and-mortar retailers are incorporating digital screens throughout stores. As you see, retailers are using digital technologies as a form of information sharing with shoppers. There are many more opportunities to utilize these technologies in store.

Below is a list of some of the most innovative ways brick-and-mortar retailers are utilizing in-store technologies:

- **In-store QR codes:** In China, supermarket Hema uses QR codes on products to inform shoppers about the dates food items were harvested, sourced, and delivered.
- **Robots:** The Hema store also includes a dining experience that uses robots to deliver meals to guests.
- **Smart shopping carts:** 7Fresh, another Chinese grocer, offers smart shopping carts that follow customers around the store. This allows customers to be hands-free, making for a more convenient shopping experience as shoppers can easily grab products from store shelves without having to worry about navigating a cart through aisles.
- **Magic mirrors:** 7Fresh also incorporates magic mirrors that display product information when it senses that items have been picked up.
- **Smart lockers:** Nike's House of Innovation 000 allows customers to reserve shoes online for in-store pick up using smart lockers. When orders are ready for pick up, shoes can be placed in a locker with the customer's name on it. Lockers can only be opened via the customer's smartphone.

- **Digital price tags:** American grocer Kroger uses digital price tags (called Kroger Edge) rather than paper tags to display pricing, promotions, and nutritional information.
- **Self-checkout:** Spanish retailer Zara introduced self-checkout, which hasn't been used much in the fashion industry as security tags make for a more complicated process. Shoppers simply hold items in front of the screen, eliminating the need to seek out and scan a barcode.
- **Mobile wallet:** Target integrated a mobile wallet within their app to make the checkout process faster and more convenient. (Target reports that using the mobile wallet is four times faster than regular payment!) To use the mobile wallet, customers use mobile devices to launch the Target app, which allows users to then scan product barcodes and make a payment using a credit card.

Throughout the text we will build upon these discussions to address how and why digital technologies are integrated throughout the brick-and-mortar shopping experience. As you read, keep in mind the retail environment will continue to evolve as customers' needs evolve. What do you think will be the next change in consumer behavior?

2.16
Self-service checkout shopping carts are offered at a supermarket in Xiangyang, Hubei Province, China. The tablet PCs installed on the handlebars of shopping carts can scan goods and allow for payments to be made.

Successes and challenges: Translating "see now, buy now" to the sales floor

Consumers' desire for immediacy has affected the fashion industry as well.

As retailers integrate a variety of platforms to engage and entice shoppers, the desire for instant gratification among consumers grows. Retailers continue to seek ways to close the gap between when clothes are shown on the runway and when they are available for purchase in their favorite stores. Many retailers have implemented, or are considering, the "see now, buy now" model.

The see now, buy now model

As consumers' demands shift to expect instant gratification with products and services, the retail industry has been working to respond to these shifts. One such way has been the "see now, buy now" trend that retailers and designers have introduced.

The **see now, buy now** trend allows customers to purchase pieces straight from the runway rather than having to wait up to six months for collection pieces to hit the sales floor. Consumers' desire for immediacy (be it food, entertainment, news, transportation, etc.), has affected the fashion industry as well. Fast fashion retail cycles have influenced the higher-end retail market; consumers have come to expect new product every week or two rather than seasonally.

However, the logistics of the "see now, buy now" trend present many challenges. Some designers and retailers are selling the runway collections solely online rather than in-store, requiring e-commerce teams to make collections available for online sales. Other retailers have made runway collections available through both e-commerce and brick-and-mortar stores. And still others are making these collections more exclusive with availability through brick-and-mortar stores only.

For example, in September 2016, Rebecca Minkoff hosted a fashion show at her SoHo boutique and customers were invited to shop the looks immediately following the show. They also live-streamed the show in augmented reality on the company's website, allowing viewers not only a 360 degree view of the stage, but also the opportunity to simply click on the model as she walked down the runway to immediately purchase any of the items. Merchandise was available for purchase in-store as well as online; the immediacy of product availability resulted in huge sales numbers for the brand. Rebecca Minkoff stated, "The first season we did this [see-now-buy-now], our sales were up 211 percent from February to February. The following season, they were up 264 percent. . ." (Petro 2018); this shows that shoppers have responded favorably to more accessible product.

Tommy Hilfiger took a similar approach as the brand created TommyNow, which is a fashion show experience that integrates the "see now, buy now" model. Throughout the fashion show, product is available as soon as the model hits the runway; product can be purchased through live-streaming of the show on the brand's website, or for fashion show attendees, they can place their orders through digital screens at the show. Introduced at New York Fashion Week in 2016, the approach has been successful for the brand and they have continued to implement the "see now, buy now" trend in their various retail outlets, including wholesale channels, social commerce channels, and their namesake stores.

Other retailers, however, take a different approach to the "see now, buy now" trend. Rather than executing a complete store overhaul, some brands set up off-site pop-up shops selling the runway collections so as to not disrupt their existing merchandising and seasonal marketing campaign.

For example, during London Fashion Week, Topshop hosted a Spring/Summer 2017 Unique Collection runway show. Immediately

2.17 and 2.18
Rebecca Minkoff's See Now, Buy Now Fashion Show at The Grove in Los Angeles, California. Guests participated in a range of activities throughout the afternoon, including a fashion show, immediately followed by shopping the newest collection.

following the show, product from the runway was available for purchase at a pop-up market. This allowed Topshop to sell different collections simultaneously, attracting the fashion leaders and influencers at the pop-up shop as well as the brand's mainstream customer at their traditional brick-and-mortar store. The pop-up shop had an air of exclusivity while the brick-and-mortar stores had the same approachable feel customers had come to expect.

Other brands and designers that have tested the "see now, buy now" format include Burberry, Ralph Lauren, Coach, and Michael Kors.

Visual merchandising teams are responsible for creating cohesion between runway shows and brick-and-mortar locations. This means bringing the runway show to life through mannequin statements, signage, interior and exterior displays and in-store merchandising; it may mean a complete store or departmental overhaul in order to fully support the featured runway collections, be it a permanent or temporary store location. These changes cannot be gradual, as with other floor sets, since the "unveiling" must be dramatic to coincide with the surprise factor of the runway shows. There cannot be any hint of the theme of the runway collection ahead of time. Additionally, existing store themes (both interior and exterior) must be removed; the current merchandise on the sales floor is moved and/or remerchandised so the focus is on the runway collection. The runway collection is merchandised in highly visible

Successes and challenges:
Translating "see now, buy now" to the sales floor, *continued*

locations on the sales floor to draw customers in and attract as much attention as possible.

Sometimes the runway collections feature merchandise that is in-season while other shows feature collections that are a season ahead (for instance, New York Fashion Week in September showcases Spring looks for the upcoming year).

Many designers and brands have switched to in-season shows as a response to changing customer behaviors. "Customers are much more interested in buying now and wearing now," said Nordstrom Inc. co-president Pete Nordstrom. "The idea that she would buy something and then put it in her closet for a couple of months until the weather changes—that has changed a lot over the years" (Milnes, 2017).

Selling in-season merchandise immediately as part of the "see now, buy now" trend allows for the sales floor to be more cohesive and complementary. Product offerings, regardless of whether they were featured on the runway or part of the seasonal collection, are likely to be complementary in terms of textures, fabrics, and silhouettes. This encourages cross-selling throughout the sales floor.

When the merchandise sold in stores is out of season, visual merchandising teams must carefully distinguish between the current season's merchandise and upcoming seasonal merchandise. The in-season merchandise appeals to the instant gratification customer whereas the "see now, buy now" merchandise from the runway appeals to the fashion leader and influencer, yet customers can easily shop from both collections.

How might the visual merchandising team differentiate between the collections?

- **Mannequin statements:** Incorporating mannequins throughout the store not only allows shoppers to envision complete looks, but can also act as dividers between

substantially different collections. Carefully placed mannequin groups subconsciously tell the shopper that they are entering a new territory with a different look and feel.
- **Fixtures:** Choosing different fixtures and/or finishes to display the different collections sends the message to shoppers that collections are housed by fixture type. For example, the in-season merchandise may be housed on 4-ways, rounders, and t-stands while the runway collection merchandise is housed on straight racks and adjacent tables. The fixtures are then grouped together, making it easy to shop each fixture of complementary merchandise.
- **Signage:** Concise and informative signage allows customers to better understand the product found on the sales floor. Incorporating consistent signage throughout the sales floor creates a sense of balance and cohesion. This is especially important when the merchandise is from different seasons.
- **Imagery:** Images can be used in a variety of ways to help tell the story of each collection. Oversized images can be used as a backdrop for the collection, showing the merchandise in advertisements, runway shows, and/or promotional materials. These images ground the collection, creating a focal point and directive for shoppers. Tabletop and fixture images also bring the collection to life, but are not quite as visible as oversized images and are more informative for shoppers in the vicinity of the fixtures. Digital imagery is another way retailers and brands can actively tell the story of the brand. Moving images may include commercials, runway shows, behind the scenes looks at the collection, as well as social media feeds. These immersive experiences allow shoppers to engage with the brand as part of the brand's storytelling efforts.

Company spotlight: 1871

1871: Chicago's Center for Technology and Entrepreneurship

Founded in 2012, 1871 is a not-for-profit organization that exists to inspire, equip, and support founders to build great businesses and connect the digital start-up community. There are nearly 500 early-stage, high-growth digital start-ups working to disrupt tired business models and challenge processes and procedures in just about any industry, from hospitality to financial services to retail. There are approximately 1,500 innovators (inventors, designers, creators) working to provide solutions to everyday problems; 1871 offers support services, ranging from a 140,000 square-foot workspace to educational lectures, mentorships, and seminars that help guide, direct, and inform its community of founders about the varied facets of their entrepreneurial ventures.

What does this mean for retail, and specifically, for visual merchandising?

> Among the 500-some start-ups at 1871, solutions are being created to develop a more streamlined, engaged, and customized shopping experience.

Among the 500-some start-ups at 1871, solutions are being created to develop a more streamlined, engaged, and customized shopping experience. Here are a couple tech entrepreneurs in 2019 that are changing the retail landscape: Meet EX3 Labs and Return Runners.

@1871CHICAGO

Meet EX3 Labs. . .

EX3 Labs is an experience design and production innovation studio that creates digital solutions for companies in order to engage customers. They work with each client to create personalized strategies to integrate immersive experiences into their business. For retail clients, EX3 Labs utilizes augmented reality and mixed reality to connect the retailer with the customer in a more holistic way. They have worked on 3D/360 space visualization, projection technology, holograms, and phone apps that incorporate virtual reality and augmented reality. These technologies benefit both front of house and back of house operations.

When looking at the back of house, we look at store planning and interior design. For store planning purposes, EX3 Labs works with real estate, construction, and store planning teams to create 3D walk-throughs of physical spaces and utilize virtual blueprints throughout the project build-out.

Using a mobile device, as the blueprint is scanned, the 2-dimensional rendering suddenly becomes a 3-dimensional room that can be explored and walked through, allowing the design team to truly experience what it is they have designed.

Here are some of the ways EX3 Labs has integrated digital experiences into the retail industry for increased customer engagement:

Space visualization

EX3 Labs has utilized different technologies for space planning projects:

360 space visualization/virtual reality
A 360-degree camera can create a realistic virtual tour for customers hoping to visit a brick-and-mortar store; they can familiarize themselves with the store ahead of time to get a better idea of store layout, merchandise, and merchandising strategies.

The 360-degree tour is also immensely beneficial during the build-out process for new store fronts, providing a way to show investors and other interested parties how a future retail space will look and feel. This experience can be integrated with 3D digital renderings to tell an even stronger story. EX3 Labs created a 3D digital rendering for partner Embarc Collective's future space in Tampa, Florida. Using Oculus Go for a virtual reality experience, EX3 Labs deployed a 3D, 360-degree visualization of the future space that also included an audio tour. This experience was designed to show investors and partners what the space will look like once it's built. The audio tour helped to explain the purpose of some of the space's unique elements.

The HoloLens

Using the HoloLens for a mixed reality experience is another great option for retail space planning. HoloLens (from Microsoft) is a mixed reality headset that allows users to interact with holograms in augmented and mixed reality. But, what does this mean?

Mixed reality allows users to see the real world around them while overlaying digital content that interacts with the physical world. In the retail environment, mixed reality is perfect for interior design and space planning.

Projection technology/augmented reality

Virtual closet? Yes! EX3 Labs leveraged projection technology, augmented reality, and depth sensor cameras to allow users to try on and plan outfits. A tiny depth sensor camera senses where the user is standing and understands their movements. Projection of augmented reality content (clothes, accessories) onto the user's reflection in the mirror allows users to see how different outfits look paired together on their body.

Mobile augmented reality

Remember Pokémon Go? No, that was not developed by EX3 Labs, but they have built other location-based apps that encourage customers to engage with brands and products on a new level. These gamified experiences for brands allow (especially younger) consumers to interact with branded content in a fun, engaging way, be it at home or in a store. Oftentimes, these experiences are games where participants use their phone to search for augmented reality content in their current environment (e.g., users have to track down their favorite candy in digital form that has been hidden around their house; upon collecting a certain amount, users earn a reward like a coupon or free product).

Another form of AR created by EX3 Labs is marker-based augmented reality apps; these add an augmented reality component to print content. For Cushman & Wakefield, a commercial real estate client, EX3 Labs created an augmented reality app to accompany their quarterly publication. This app enabled readers to use their phone to recognize certain pages of the publication to activate digital content. This brought the print media to life, as users connected with Cushman & Wakefield to virtually to hear a video address from the CEO, 3D visualizations of buildings, and 3D charts and graphs appeared, to name a few.

From a visual merchandising and marketing perspective, these immersive technologies create awareness, enhance brand loyalty, and build relationships through interactive experiences.

Meet ReturnRunners

Have you ever purchased something and then realized you won't actually ever wear it? Blame it on the fitting room lighting or "trick" mirror; or maybe it was an impulse purchase; or something you already have too many of in your existing wardrobe. Whatever the reason, it needs to be returned. The problem? There are only so many hours in the day and you won't have a chance to run back to the store or box it up and mail it back.

Product returns were estimated to be close to $400 billion in 2018; the return process is overwhelming for both retailers and customers. Not only are retailers dealing with product returns in the short-term (adhering to their designated return window timeframe), but they are also dealing with the potential of lost sales in the long-term. If the return process is too cumbersome or frustrating, shoppers will seek alternative retailers from which to make purchases the next time around. From a consumer perspective, missing the allotted timeframe for a return means wasted money and unwanted clutter at home, neither of which is well-received.

Cue ReturnRunners. Founded in 2017, ReturnRunners is all about eliminating the hassles of returning unwanted merchandise. ReturnRunners creates a frictionless return experience so users can complete their return without having to leave their house. Users download an app that will connect them with a company "runner." The digital platform allows the users to choose a convenient pick up time and location in which to meet their runner; the runner then completes the return, either at brick-and-mortar stores or by packaging and shipping online orders back. Users receive updates throughout the process, sending a confirmation upon completion of the return. ReturnRunners customers can expect to see refunds from the returned items in 2–3 business days.

From a business perspective, the partnership between retailers and ReturnRunners enhances the relationship between retailers and customers because of increased brand engagement. Retailers are utilizing the services of ReturnRunners to meet the changing needs of customers, creating a more convenient shopping experience.

Summary

Visual merchandising has evolved from simply product placement to interactive and immersive displays. As consumer lifestyles change, retailers must adapt the store environment to meet these changes. With the continued innovation in digital technologies, retailers work to integrate digital aspects throughout the shopping experience, ranging from omnichannel platforms to digital signage and experiential retail. Shoppers engage with brands through product customization, "try before you buy," and brand storytelling, to name a few. The retail environment is constantly changing, and as a result, store displays, both interior and exterior, will continue to change in order to create a loyal customer base.

KEY TERMS

Connected fitting room
Conversational commerce
E-commerce
Multi-channel retail
Omnichannel retail
RFID
S-commerce
See now, buy now
Smart mirror

CRITICAL THINKING: THE APPLICATION PROCESS

After completing the chapter readings, reflect on the information and experiences shared. Apply what you learned to future retail experiences:

1. What are some advantages and disadvantages for customers to use in-store technologies to complete their purchases?
2. Window installations and in-store experiences often feel like tourist attractions, drawing in an audience. How do retailers turn these free "attractions" into sales?
3. What is the role of the visual merchandiser in the "see now, buy now" trend?
4. What components would you find beneficial within a smart mirror?

3

Visual merchandising and omnichannel retail

Overview

Today's shoppers are accustomed to information at their fingertips; they seek information from a variety of sources before finalizing a purchase. Omnichannel retail offers a seamless experience across channels and devices, allowing shoppers to access information when and where it is convenient for them; however, messaging on one channel and/or device must be consistent when shoppers move to the next device to continue their shopping. It is imperative that visual merchandisers are aware of brand messaging across platforms to create a cohesive in-store experience. A recent development is also that visual merchandisers seek opportunities to integrate digital technologies throughout displays in order to effectively communicate with shoppers. Some examples of these technologies include location-based services, beacon technologies, interactive displays, and mass customization opportunities.

3.1
Today's shoppers have the ability to browse merchandise virtually from anywhere they choose, make a purchase, then stop into their local store to pick up their purchase.

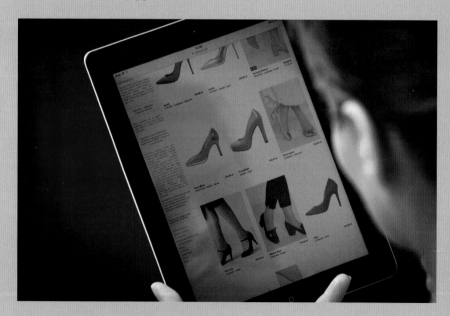

Enhancing the online shopping experience

In 2017, the phrase "retail apocalypse" was heard time and time again; each time a retailer closed their doors, it appeared to support the notion that retail was, in fact, dying. However, the truth is, retail sales were actually on the rise. According to *The Wall Street Journal*, total retail sales grew 4.2 percent in calendar year 2017(Chaney and Mitchell, 2017). What this tells us is that brick-and-mortar retailers were not shutting their doors because consumers were no longer spending. The shuttering of brick-and-mortar stores was a result of buyer behavior—people were shopping differently.

As new digital technologies are continually introduced, shoppers are finding new platforms in which to shop, research, connect, and engage with retailers and brands. Today's shoppers are accustomed to information at their fingertips; they seek information from a variety of sources before finalizing a purchase. In fact, according to Deloitte Consulting, digital interactions influence 56 cents of every dollar spent in brick-and-mortar stores (Deloitte 2016). In order to appeal to the changing shopping habits of consumers, retailers built omnichannel retail experiences. As you learned in Chapter 2, omnichannel retail offers a seamless experience across various channels and devices, allowing shoppers to access information when and where it is convenient for them. Retailers no longer view online and brick-and-mortar shopping as separate divisions; they can, should, and oftentimes are now integrated into one.

Farfetch, a luxury fashion retailer, has done just that. In April 2017, Farfetch launched a truly immersive, omnichannel retail experience, linking the online and offline shopping experience in their London store. Farfetch uses connected clothing racks, touchscreen-enhanced mirrors, and sign-in stations to connect shoppers in the physical store location to their online accounts. The

3.2
Farfetch U.K. Ltd.'s Store Of The Future. A touchscreen mirror displays a welcome message and displays a consumer's product choices at the launch of the Farfetch U.K. Ltd. "Store of the Future" pop-up exhibition, at the Design Museum in London, U.K.

sign-in stations allow customers to access their online accounts to search their purchase history and bucket list while simultaneously working with in-store associates, providing important customer insight for the sales associates to better assist shoppers. The touchscreen mirrors allow shoppers to request different sizes, alternative products, or complete the checkout process without leaving the dressing room. Additional in-store technologies give customers the opportunity to customize and order shoes with different styles and fabrics.

The innovative shopping experience offered at Farfetch enables each customer to enjoy a customized shopping experience based on their individual shopping habits. This one-of-a-kind experience blends the conveniences of both boutique shopping and online shopping into one.

This is one example of just how far retailers are reaching to integrate the online and in-store experiences, incentivizing customers to shop the various platforms simultaneously by providing a seamless shopping experience from one platform to the next.

3.3
Niketown's in-store shopping experience is highly integrated with their app to encourage customers to connect digitally to create a more convenient, seamless shopping experience. The in-store pick up area for shoppers who made a purchase through the Nike app is clearly labeled for a convenient final step in the purchase process.

But, what does this mean for consumers? How are the digital and in-store experiences supporting one another, and what does this mean for visual merchandisers? As you will see, omnichannel doesn't mean just one thing for all retailers. There are different ways to integrate the physical and virtual shopping experiences.

Here are a few examples of what we see in the current marketplace; what others should be included?

- *Buy online, pick up in-store*: Customers can make a purchase from various devices (mobile device, tablet, desktop, laptop, etc.) and then pick up their purchases in-store rather than have the product shipped to their home. This could save time, shipping costs, and/or offer added security for shoppers who don't want packages sent to their home.

  Visual Merchandising Implications: The "buy online, pick up in-store" experience creates a convenient shopping option for customers, but nothing is more frustrating than arriving at the store and not knowing where to pick up your order. Visual merchandisers must use clear, concise, and highly visual signage as in-store directives. This ensures the in-store pick up is as convenient as placing the online order was. It is also a great opportunity to up-sell customers. Remember when we said the biggest challenge retailers face is getting customers into their stores? Well, the "buy online, pick up in store" option has gotten the customer into the store; it is now up to the visual merchandising team to provide clear messaging and introduce complementary products through product adjacencies, styling, and effective merchandising strategies.

- *Shop online, Reserve in-store:* Shoppers find merchandise online and are interested in seeing it, touching it, and/or trying it on before making a purchase. Rather than visiting the store and having to seek it out, the "reserve" option allows shoppers to place the merchandise on hold for them to stop in and try on at their convenience.

Visual Merchandising Implications: As with the "buy online, pick up in-store" option, messaging for the "reserve in-store" experience must be clear so shoppers know where their product(s) will be held. Additionally, retailers have now gotten customers into the store; this is an opportunity to suggestive-sell before the customer heads to the fitting room. Now is the time to help shoppers complete the look, just as conveniently as their "reserve in-store" option was. Window displays, interior installations, and mannequins quickly inform customers of head-to-toe looks. Remember that these customers are not visiting the stores with the intention to shop the fixtures; effective merchandising strategies entice these shoppers to take a few extra minutes to grab products that will complement their purchase.

- *In-store tablets*: Retailers are incorporating tablets into the in-store shopping experience in order to accomplish a variety of tasks and offer new opportunities for shoppers. In-store tablets allow customers to shop the retailer's e-commerce sites and take advantage of increased inventory levels, as opposed to being limited by square footage for their merchandise assortment. E-commerce sites offer endless aisles; endless aisles offer greater merchandise assortment, giving shoppers a wider range of sizes, colors, and styles. In-store tablets oftentimes allow shoppers to customize products, changing colors and patterns, adding monograms or messages, and/or incorporating embellishments and other details. This allows customers to feel like they are purchasing one-of-a-kind products that cannot be found elsewhere; it also reduces product returns, as customized products are non-returnable! Lastly, the customization of products gives retailers the opportunity to engage customers in the design and purchasing processes as

it provides market research about what customers are looking for and willing to purchase.

Another use for in-store tablets and screens is strictly informational. Brands and retailers can showcase marketing campaigns and fashion shows, and provide product knowledge and styling recommendations that act as suggestive selling tools and demonstrate product benefits. This highly visual tool not only provides the opportunity to show off additional merchandise, but it also eliminates clutter on the sales floor, saving valuable space for customers to move around. Using tablets for information sharing reduces clunky signage as retailers can also take advantage of the flexibility of digital signage to show products being used in real-life situations, quickly adapting and updating messaging at a moment's notice.

Visual Merchandising Implications: Tablets must be easily accessible and placed in a high traffic area. This ensures that customers know the tablet is for public use. Visual merchandisers should also utilize a stand or fixture that keeps the tablet waist-high so it is easy for customers to access the web page and see the screen. If the intended use is for product customization, it is important that visual merchandisers place corresponding product on an adjacent fixture or table, if possible, so customers can touch, feel, and analyze the product as they build out their customization, enabling shoppers to make informed decisions for their customizations (as customized products typically are not returnable). Additionally, fixture and product placement should include the various color options, complementary products, and informational signage. The customization process should not require oversight from a sales associate; if questions continually arise, the retailer has not included sufficient informative signage.

3.4
At Roots stores, fitting rooms feature mounted iPads that
are connected to the brand's e-commerce site. Customers
are encouraged to continue shopping the site, which offers
a broader assortment of products than in-store offerings.
Shoppers can take their time exploring the site.

- *Up-to-date inventory levels and in-store
  location*: When shoppers prefer to make a
  purchase in-store rather than wait for the
  product(s) to be shipped, e-commerce sites
  can provide information about in-store
  availability, saving customers from making
  a trip to the store only to leave empty-
  handed. Radio frequency identification
  (RFID) tags enable retailers to provide
  live updates on inventory levels, letting
  shoppers know if the very product they
  are looking for is available for purchase
  at a nearby store location. If there are
  several retail locations in close proximity,
  e-commerce sites can provide information
  about the inventory levels at the different
  locations, letting shoppers know which
  location is most likely to have what they

are looking for. Retail websites can offer
information about not only inventory
levels, but also where to find the product
within the brick-and-mortar store. This
creates a convenient in-store shopping
experience because shoppers know the
exact location (department, aisle, or store
location) for finding the product rather
than having to navigate and explore the
entire store and/or visit multiple store
locations.

  Visual merchandising implications:
Visual merchandising teams and
e-commerce teams must be in constant
communication to ensure that information
is accurate and up-to-date. Product is
continually remerchandised to keep
the sales floor looking full and product
assortment fresh; as product is moved
around, there are implications for the
digital shopping experience as well. If
a product is relocated on the sales floor,
the online information must be updated
to ensure customers receive accurate
information for a successful omnichannel
experience.

- *Schedule an appointment through
  retailer's app or website*: Customers can
  use a retailer's app to schedule in-store
  appointments for a more convenient
  shopping experience. Shoppers are
  guaranteed appointments with their
  stylist, sales associate, tailor, or
  customer service team member. This
  ensures that they have dedicated time
  set aside, alleviating the wait time.
  Apple is incredibly successful in using
  their websites to secure one-on-one
  appointments with customers in-store at
  their Genius Bar. Shoppers visit apple.
  com, choose the store location of their
  choice, pick an available timeslot, and
  know exactly when they need to arrive at
  the store based on a mutually agreed upon
  time. With the click of a button, they have
  secured the expertise of an Apple Genius,
  eliminating the sit-and-wait model. While
  in-store for their appointment at the
  Genius Bar, shoppers are immersed in the

retail environment, exposed to the energy, excitement, and slew of other products and services offered by the retailer. It is a safe bet that before or after their Genius Bar appointment, shoppers take time to explore the Apple store, products, services, and event happenings.

- *Guideshop:* E-commerce retailers have recognized the importance of physical store locations, but are often reluctant to implement a full-scale retail operation. Instead, brands are setting up guideshops. **Guideshops** require much smaller physical footprints because stores do not carry complete size runs and comprehensive inventory levels. There is a size run for try-on purposes only, allowing customers to touch, feel, and try on merchandise, get sized, and talk to a sales associate before placing orders. Orders are placed through the brand's e-commerce site before the customer leaves the guideshop and are shipped directly to the customers' home. This model offers a mutually beneficial shopping experience,

as customers are able to try on products and compare sizes before committing to a purchase, reducing product returns back to the brand. Bonobos, a contemporary men's retailer, successfully transitioned from an e-tailer to opening close to fifty guideshops throughout the United States. Bonobos found that the average in-store order size is twice that of online orders, customers are more likely to make repeat transactions, and they acquire a higher number of new customers coming through their physical channel.

Visual merchandising implications: Guideshops provide a physical location to bring the virtual shopping experience to life. The in-store experience is an opportunity to create a comprehensive brand experience, integrating the sensory retail experience with the brand's product offering. Brands create the comprehensive brand experience through choice of fixtures, furniture, and displays, coupled with in-store playlists, scents, and on-brand customer service.

3.5
General view of Bonobos Guideshop. As you see, guideshops don't display full size runs of their merchandise. Shoppers work closely with stylists who pull sizes to try on from the back room; the products are for try-on purposes only. Once customers and stylists determine the best fit, the products are ordered online and shipped to the customer's home.

As you see, omnichannel retail doesn't mean just one thing; it is constantly evolving as new platforms and technologies are introduced to the marketplace. There are many examples of retailers that are effectively utilizing omnichannel, but others are simply operating as multichannel retailers. Effective omnichannel retail captures shoppers across platforms, creating a convenient shopping experience for customers whenever and wherever they are. (Multichannel retailers, on the other hand, have a retail presence on various platforms, allowing customers to shop from mobile devices, computers, catalog, etc. However, these platforms are not synched with one another. When a customer shops from their desktop computer, their shopping cart will not reappear when they open the same retailer's app or mobile-friendly website on a different device.)

American home improvement store Home Depot is a great example of a big box retailer that effectively utilizes omnichannel. They have integrated their online and brick-and-mortar shopping experiences into one cohesive experience as they invite customers to use their website and mobile app prior to visiting brick-and-mortar stores in order to help shoppers better navigate their massive stores. A customer can load their virtual shopping cart with their shopping needs prior to visiting a store. Then when they enter the brick-and-mortar store and launch the Home Depot mobile app, the app will direct them to the corresponding aisle and shelf for the exact items in their virtual cart. When the shopper finds the aisle and shelf location, the identifying location information that is communicated via the e-commerce site and mobile app is also displayed on the shelving unit to ensure the correct product is placed in one's physical shopping cart.

This gets the online shopper into Home Depot stores, not only assisting them with their shopping needs, but also exposing them to the thousands of other products available for purchase as there are hundreds (if not thousands) of complementary products merchandised in close proximity. Add-on purchases are almost guaranteed. Shopping in-store also connects shoppers to knowledgeable sales associates who can provide assistance and advice for home projects.

The biggest challenge with omnichannel retail is that messaging and information shared must be consistent from one platform to the next; each platform cannot feel like a completely different retailer or shopping experience, as customers will be confused. For the brick-and-mortar customer, visual merchandisers must thoughtfully integrate digital technologies throughout displays in order to effectively communicate and/or reinforce digital messages to shoppers. For the online shopper, the brick-and-mortar experience must replicate the digital experience in terms of not only brand messaging but also convenience.

The digital messages shared varies from one retailer to the next and from one season to the next, but typically these digital technologies share brands' and retailers' social media feeds, behind the scenes process work, and e-commerce sites.

3.6
Aisle and shelf locations are carefully labeled throughout Home Depot stores, making it easy for their online customers to identify the exact location of merchandise they have added to their virtual shopping cart before visiting a brick-and-mortar store to make an in-store purchase.

Integrating social media moments into visual merchandising

Retailers are creating social media moments throughout the store to encourage social media posts and photo sharing to increase awareness of trends, product offerings, and the brand itself.

With the growing presence of omnichannel retail, retailers and brands are also seeking ways to connect with customers in an organic, unobtrusive manner. Social media has done just that: provide an outlet for retailers, brands, and customers to communicate with each other, sharing both brand- and user-generated content to their respective networks of followers.

In 2019, 79 percent of US adults had active social media accounts, providing a platform for customers to share photos and experiences, ask questions, and engage with their favorite brands (Clement, 2020). Social media platforms like Instagram, Twitter, Facebook, YouTube, and TikTok provide a platform for consumers to share product reviews, brand experiences, both in-store and online, and demonstrate product usage, be it positive or negative, with the brands as well as their network of followers. This user-generated content greatly impacts a potential customer's decision as to whether or not to make a future purchase. Social media can also provide another platform for customers to make a purchase, capturing followers to conveniently purchase an array of products with a quick click of a button. As you learned earlier in the text, shopping via social media is the newest form of e-commerce, referred to as s-commerce.

Why is this important? Well, it tells brands and retailers about the sheer number of people who have social media accounts as well as how and where users are accessing these accounts. Users are increasingly logging into social media accounts through their smartphones, creating a demand for brands to connect to their on-the-go customers.

Retailers have taken note and are integrating social media into the shopping experience.

Effective use of social media brings us back to Chapter 2 and our discussion of brand storytelling; social media posts, stories, and hashtags can provide an up-to-the minute story about the brand experience, events, and activities. This allows users and shoppers to better understand what the brand stands for, community engagement, behind-the-scenes process work, and photo shoots and fashion shows, to name a few. These all reinforce the brand's storytelling.

These stories are comprised of both brand-generated and user-generated content, both of which are important to the sales process. **Brand-generated content** is part of the brand marketing; **user-generated content**, on the other hand, is content posted and shared by customers. Brand-generated content is created and pushed out through the brand's marketing channels. User-generated content is created by brand and product customers sharing their experiences and feedback from what appears to be a more honest approach.

3.7
Tory Burch reinforces brand messaging by directing shoppers to social media to connect with the brand through a themed hashtag.

Just how important is social media to product sales? Well, 74 percent of shoppers prioritize feedback found on social media. Opinions from family, friends, and influencers guide and inform them in their decision-making process (Digital Marketing Institute, 2019). Shoppers are reviewing product ratings, written reviews, and product Q&A's before finalizing purchases.

What does this mean? Recommendations from one's personal connections or social media influencers tend to be more effective than paid marketing messages. Social media is an opt-in experience; users have voluntarily chosen to connect with a brand by following them. Social media is also a platform for word-of-mouth marketing, allowing users to share images, products, and experiences with their networks or post directly to a brand's page with the click of a button. This information often feels more authentic as it is not coming from the brand itself.

Brands and retailers have no control over user-generated content but they are working hard to subtly guide users in the messages shared via social media. TikTok is one such platform retailers are using to direct user-generated content messaging. Popular with Generation Z consumers, TikTok is a social media platform centered around video sharing. Macy's utilized TikTok in their 2019 Back-to-School programming as they invited teens to show off their back-to-school apparel, accessory, beauty, and dorm purchases through singing, dancing, and tagging #AllBrandNew. Although these videos are not completed in-store, consider how retailers can activate these social media challenges in-store as well. Retailers and visual merchandising teams are taking steps to curate social media moments in-store, in hopes that shoppers will help them tell their (un)branded story.

Did you know that people are accessing 69 percent of their media on their smartphones? (Sterling, 2017)

How do visual merchandisers guide the social media messaging?

Accessibility

Instagram is the most highly visual social media site and has become the most widely used visual storyteller for brands. As of 2020, over 40 billion photos have been shared on Instagram (Social Media Perth, 2020).

Visual merchandising teams are creating highly accessible Instagram moments for quick, easy, and convenient social media posts.

In order for retailers to create Instagram-ready displays, they are using square-ready formats for both interior and exterior displays. Additionally, store window displays are continually changed to keep up with consumer demands.

3.8
An Instagram-ready interior display invites shoppers to snap a quick photo while shopping; the square-shaped vignettes make it easy for shoppers to take photos that fit into the Instagram format. There is no editing needing before sharing the image across social media platforms.

What does that mean? Visual merchandising teams are creating Instagram-ready displays in 3 steps:

1. **Shape:** Using square-shaped displays eliminates the need for shoppers to crop and edit photos of the displays.
2. **Adaptability:** No longer featuring time intensive displays, displays are adaptable, addressing time-sensitive trends and fickle customers!
3. **Hashtags:** Concise, catchy, and informative hashtags increase followers and complete the story being told.

From a consumer perspective, when a retailer adheres to these guidelines, documenting the Instagram moment is quick. Creating Instagram moments for shoppers eliminates the need for shoppers to crop, rotate, and edit images before sharing with their Instagram followers. Instead, with a click of a button, the retailer's brand image and merchandise offerings are shared globally, with subtle oversight from the retailer.

For example, Podolyan, a store in Kiev, Russia, effectively created Instagram moments for shoppers by merchandising product in grid-like form to align with Instagram's format. The grid showcased new, on-trend merchandise, creating a visual prompt for shoppers to snap a photo and share it with their networks. It was a subtle call-to-action for shoppers that required little to no effort in terms of editing because the grid allowed images to fit perfectly within the Instagram format, reiterating the very design that the merchandising team created.

From a business perspective, Podolyan's merchandising strategy made it easy for visual

3.9
A yellow bicycle promotes the L'Occitane en Provence brand. At the Aspen, Colorado, store, the bicycle is propped outside the store to generate awareness; other store locations have included the yellow bicycle in varied locations, both inside and outside the stores.

merchandising teams to dictate the story being told at a moment's notice. The grid allowed them quickly swap out product based on inventory levels as well as to ensure they were adhering to the newest trends in order to tell a current, relevant story.

Another way to create Instagram moments is by featuring installations that invite shoppers to hop in and be part of the installation and/or image. These installations are designed with the user in mind, clearly designating where the shopper should go for the best social media photo op, creating shareable experiences for customers.

For example, L'Occitane en Provence's flagship store took advantage of an underutilized area of the store to create a social media experience for their shoppers. They hung an image of a cobblestone street in Provence, lined with charming buildings and lots of greenery; they then strategically placed three cheery yellow bicycles in front of the graphic, inviting customers to immerse themselves in the city of Provence by hopping on the bikes, playing around, and snapping a

few photos. These photos were automatically uploaded to the retailer's live Instagram feed, which was projected adjacent to the backdrop. As shoppers saw the feed instantly updated, they were more inclined to join in on the fun. . . and follow the brand's social media so they could tag themselves and share the photos with their friends.

British retailer Ted Baker ran a Merry Kissmas campaign that invited customers to take selfies under a large digital mistletoe installation, use #KissTed, and share it with friends. The incentive? The images were featured on a digital display on top of the store entrances to the Ted Baker stores on Fifth Avenue in New York City, in London's Westfield shopping center, and Tokyo's Omotesando shopping street. Rather than the typical images of models in marketing campaigns, actual customers became the stars of the holiday campaign, creating a connection with the brand among their global customer base. An added incentive for using the #KissTed? The Merry Kissmas campaign also promoted a chance for participants to win a vacation for two! This demonstrates how retailers are using hashtags to encourage shoppers to share messages, images, and videos in order to qualify for free product, discounted prices, or limited edition wares.

Retailers are also dedicating entire walls and/or windows to their social media feeds, most often featuring a live Instagram feed. Not only does this promote brand loyalty by encouraging shoppers to follow the brand on various social media platforms, but it also provides a sense of reality. Shoppers are able to see how actual customers use products and incorporate them into their daily routines. In return, shoppers are anxious for their "fifteen minutes of fame" and are more likely to take photos, utilize hashtags, and tag the retailer or brand in order to see their images featured on the retailer's wall.

Hashtags

Hashtags are an easy way for retailers to connect the online and in-store shopping experiences. Branded hashtags can be both permanent and temporary as it could simply be the brand's name or signature tagline (permanent) or reflective of a seasonal

trend or campaign (temporary, as seen with #KissTed). Hashtags make for an easy transition from in-store to online conversations and participation. Shoppers can join these conversations and learn more about the brand, store, customers, and/or branded events. Retailers and brands choose to use branded hashtags to track shared messages and overall reach.

Vineyard Vines, a popular American brand for the preppy Millennial crowd, incorporates #EDSFTG (Everyday Should Feel This Good) in all their social media posts and marketing collateral, including store displays, as this is an important tagline for their branding. However, hashtags are also fluid and new ones can be introduced at a moment's notice as a tie-in to a holiday, event, or collaboration. For example, in 2018, to celebrate their twentieth anniversary, Vineyard Vines introduced #vineyardvines20years; this was used temporarily in addition to #EDSFTG. These hashtags were integrated throughout social media, print marketing, and interior and exterior displays, including window displays. These hashtags can also be used to engage with customers throughout their

3.10
Hashtags act as an easy reminder for customers to connect with brands on social media sites to be informed, entertained, and inspired. From a business perspective, hashtags allow retailers and brands to track activity and gain insights into their followers.

shopping experience, providing a call-to-action to share experiences, store images, and product offerings through their social media sites, reaching both new and current customers. Vineyard Vines encourages their customers to post photos in their Vineyard Vines merchandise and incorporate #EDSFTG for easy tracking from the brand and their followers. Retailers may include hashtags and social media icons as directives in store windows by featuring hashtags on windowpanes, oversized graphics, or even live social media feeds.

Product callout

Lastly, visual merchandisers can rely on the power of social influencers to impact in-store buying decisions. Social media posts, specifically by influencers, create an instant demand for products. However, even if shoppers are not seeking information on social media, social media content can be brought to them throughout their in-store shopping experience.

One way retailers are bringing social media to their customers is through projecting live social media feeds within the store to create awareness of seasonal trends and product offerings. These live feeds feature rotating images that appeal to an array of customers. Shoppers are able to seek inspiration for how to wear and/or style garments; they are also able to see product in use, on an actual body. In-store social media feeds also act as a reminder to customers to share their looks on social media with corresponding tags as a form of word-of-mouth advertising since user-generated social media content feels more genuine than a brand-sponsored advertisement.

Another way social media is integrated into the in-store experience is through product call-outs. Retailers can (and should) merchandise their stores to feature "top pinned" sections that reference the social media site Pinterest. The merchandise would vary based on seasonal trends and engagement on social media. For example,

Nordstrom incorporated Pinterest's iconic logo on the sales floor to highlight products that gained popularity on the social media site. Product that gained popularity on Pinterest was designated with "Most Pinned" tags on the sales floor. This was a great way to call attention to what is relevant on social media in relation to the Nordstrom target consumer. Shoppers immediately took notice and were made aware of social trends, creating a sense of community and reinforcing a feeling of acceptance. The small but noticeable signage on merchandise also attracted customers who may not have otherwise showed interest in the product.

Architecture

Retailers are integrating unique architectural elements into store designs to generate excitement, both for the physical store and throughout social media. These brick-and-mortar stores become shopping destinations to, primarily, experience these architectural elements, and, as a secondary, customers then shop the store.

3.11
This oversized bust form at the Under Armour Brand House in Chicago is built into the store design, creating a focal point for customers and passersby alike. Shoppers have a hard time resisting the photo op and sharing it with their networks.

The Under Armour Brand House on Chicago's Magnificent Mile greets customers with a massive bust form with #UACHICAGO splashed across the chest. The larger-than-life installation is highly visible from the street and is often surrounded by shoppers and tourists alike who line up to snap a photo. By tagging the photo with #UACHICAGO, users are instantly featured on digital screens surrounding the form as well as throughout the brand's social media feed. Customers spend time sifting through the photos that are continually posted to the feed, connecting with the array of shoppers who visited the brand house.

Product plus store design

Retailers are also utilizing in-store installations that integrate architectural elements and merchandise to garner attention across social media platforms. New York City's streetwear store Kith partnered with Snarkitecture for an in-store installation that generates a lot of buzz both for the product and the installation itself. Immediately upon entering Kith, shoppers are greeted by an installation of hundreds of white cast-replica Nike Air Jordan II's encased in a glass tunnel-like installation in the floor. The monochromatic color story and repetition make a strong impact, both promoting the sneakers as well as providing a photo opportunity.

Instagram Checkout

Social commerce, as mentioned earlier, is the use of social networking sites as a selling platform; it allows participants, both companies and customers, to buy and sell products electronically. Instagram Checkout is a feature that was added to the social media platform in 2019 in order to make it even more convenient for Instagram users to make a purchase.

Prior to the launch of Instagram Checkout, Instagram users were able to shop through the social media site, but it was a cumbersome process. If users were interested in a product, they could click through on product tags, eventually being taken to the brands' website via the web browsers to complete their purchase. This was time consuming and often lost shoppers throughout the process. With Instagram Checkout, Instagram users save credit card information and a shipping address, so when they are ready to make a purchase, it is a seamless process as the transaction is completed directly through Instagram rather than being redirected to a retailer's site. As retailers and brands build out their presence on Instagram to create awareness of both products and branded lifestyle, the social media site is no longer just for seeking inspiration; it is now another selling platform.

What does this mean for visual merchandisers? As displays are created to target the brick-and-mortar shoppers, these same displays can be photographed and uploaded to Instagram, with products tagged, allowing for in-app shopping. Shoppers can shop directly through the Instagram app for a seamless shopping experience.

3.12 and 3.13
Kith created a social media moment in-store through a
permanent installation featuring replicas of product sold at
the store. The installation serves dual purposes as not only are
shoppers sharing photos of the installation with their social
media connections, but they are also increasing awareness of
Nike Air Jordan IIs.

Integrating mobile devices into the shopping experience

According to a 2019 study by Pew Research Center, approximately 81 percent of Americans own a smartphone; this makes the smartphone one of the most quickly adopted consumer technologies in recent history. The same Pew Research Center study found that 59 percent of US adults have used their cell phone to call or text someone while inside a store to discuss purchases they are thinking of making; 45 percent of US adults have used their phones while inside a store to look up online reviews or to try and competitive shop for something they are thinking of purchasing. A relatively small share of Americans (12 percent) have used their cell phones to physically pay for in-store purchases.

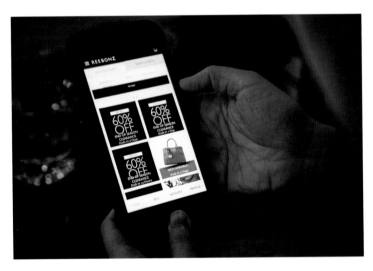

3.14
Smartphones are used throughout the shopping experience for product information, customer reviews, and promotional information.

Simply using a smartphone has added a lot of opportunity for both retailers and customers. The checkout process has become streamlined; there does not need to be a separate sales associate or point-of-sale (POS) system to ring up sales. Retailers are able to push information to customers through their mobile app; displays and mannequins are able to inform customers of product offerings and in-store location through both digital and physical signage; interactive displays allow customers to connect and engage with the brand, building long-term relationships and brand awareness. Apps provide information on navigating the store by providing maps.

Smartphones and mobile devices are often used as part of the brick-and-mortar shopping experience, both by retailers and shoppers. Today's shoppers have become accustomed to the integration of mobile devices in the brick-and-mortar shopping experience. Not only do we see customers using their mobile devices to shop and research *while* shopping at brick-and-mortar stores, but retailers are also incorporating mobile devices in the selling and merchandising of products in their brick-and-mortar stores.

Bulky cash wraps are no longer necessary on the retail sales floor. The sales floor now features tablets and/or sales associates armed with mobile devices to streamline the checkout process. Sales can be completed where and when it is most convenient for the customer. This frees up more space for merchandise, in-store experiences, digital technologies, and seating areas.

3.15
Instagram-driven makeup brand Glossier hosted a pop-up shop in Boston's Seaport District. The digitally native brand emphasized in-store experiences for shoppers, eliminating cash wraps. Instead, customers were directed outside the Glossier pop-up shops to pick up their orders.

Perhaps the most common use of mobile devices by retailers is as a replacement for the cash register. Retailers are bringing the POS system directly to the customer by using tablets to ring up customers wherever the customers may be. This eliminates customers having to wait in line, as today's instant gratification customers don't want to wait for anything! But more importantly, the elimination of a cash wrap frees up valuable selling space for the retailer to utilize. From a visual merchandising perspective, the cash wrap acted as a last attempt to upsell customers on merchandise. Think about the last time you were rung up at a cash register; you likely were surrounded by point-of-purchase (POP) merchandise, quick and easy add-ons at a relatively low price point. Where are these products now merchandised to entice customers to make convenient (i.e., effortless) last minute purchases?

Retailers are also using mobile devices to improve the in-store customer service experience. Nordstrom, an American specialty retailer best known for their superior customer service, is utilizing mobile devices throughout the customer shopping experience to create a more informed and personalized shopping experience. In-store sales associates are provided mobile devices that provide digital store layouts and product knowledge for merchandise found within their store location. As a result, when sales associates are stopped by customers with an inquiry, Nordstrom employees can seek out the necessary information with the swipe of a screen, rather than direct shoppers to Customer Service desks or the nearest in-store directory. These same devices act as mobile point-of-sale systems, allowing the checkout process to be completed anywhere within the store.

In 2018, Nordstrom showed shoppers, yet again, how brick-and-mortar retailers remain relevant in a time when opportunities for online shopping continue to increase. Nordstrom acquired BevyUp, a retail technology company, whose services enable Nordstrom employees to connect with their customers twenty-four hours a day, seven days a week. Using the Nordstrom employee app, the BevyUp Style Board allows Nordstrom stylists to send their customers product recommendations based on their purchase history. For customers, knowing that their Nordstrom stylist is accessible via mobile device creates a stronger personal connection. No longer are customers dialing into a switchboard to have their stylist paged; they can simply open their Nordstrom app, email, or instant messages to learn about new trends and products that fit their lifestyle. And making a purchase is just a click away.

Apps

Nike is another brand that continues to use new technologies to provide interactive, innovative experiences for their customers. Niketown stores dedicate floor and fixture space to promote the use of the Nike Fit app in order to create a seamless shopping experience between the physical and digital retail outlets. As shoppers walk through the doors into the store, wall signage informs them of the benefits received by downloading the Nike app. This is reinforced throughout the store on fixtures and tables. By downloading the app, shoppers have increased access to merchandise, as well as product knowledge, without relying on sales associates.

In 2019, Nike enhanced the Nike Fit app to include augmented reality scanning to measure the size and shape of one's feet in order to identify the best size and style of shoe for the customer. Using the camera of a smartphone, the app scans thirteen data points on each foot; this information is stored in the member's NikePlus profile. Armed with these detailed measurements, when the user

3.16 and 3.17
While shopping Niketown brick-and-mortar stores, shoppers are encouraged to use the Nike Fit app to enhance their shopping experience and relationship to the brand.

visits a Nike store, a sales associate can scan a QR code in the app to see which shoes are the best fit for the customer. The integration of the Nike app and brick-and-mortar shopping keeps customers connected to the brand through multiple touch points. The customer who uses and/or shops Nike through digital platforms is directed to the store to complete their purchase and connect with a sales associate; the brick-and-mortar customer is encouraged to connect with Nike through the app, where they can complete a comprehensive customer profile and will be notified of relevant product offerings and events.

Utilizing augmented reality to identify the best size and type of shoe is incredibly important as online shoppers are often unsure what size shoe to order, as there is no consistency from one brand to the next. According to Nike, more than 60 percent of people are wearing the wrong shoe size. Knowing they are ordering a shoe that is guaranteed to fit reduces product returns and customer frustration. Additionally, when using the Nike Fit app, users are presented with the most relevant products based on their profile, including sizing, which likely exposes the customer to additional products for future sales that are sure to fit.

Retailers like Walmart are inviting customers to use store apps to provide assistance navigating their massive stores. The Walmart app includes a store map for each Walmart store location, allowing customers to familiarize themselves with the store before arriving, helping them shop quickly and more efficiently. The map shows an item's exact location and is specific to the store location chosen by the customer. As product offerings continually change, the in-store map ensures customers know exactly where to locate merchandise before stepping foot in the store.

Lush Cosmetics, best known for their sustainable and ethical practices, relies on digital technologies to provide product information typically found on product packaging. Lush touts that 35 percent of their products are sold sans packaging, supporting their mission of "reducing our waste wherever possible." (In fact, they recently opened a packaging-free store in Manchester to reinforce their stance on environmental practices.) However, packaging is where customers are able to glean information about ingredients, usage, benefits, etc. To ensure that customers are not missing out, this information can now be accessed through the Lush Lens app. When customers scan the product in the Lush Lens app, machine learning is used to recognize the product and then share product information. **Machine learning** falls under the realm of artificial intelligence. Machine learning is the process of computers (aka machines) collecting information through observations and real-world interactions with its users. As a result of these interactions, the computer is able to make informed, relevant recommendations for products and services. The more interactions between the user and computer, the more relevant their recommendations will be. Machine learning is a suggestive sales tool.

These are just a few examples depicting how retailers are utilizing apps to enhance the in-store shopping experience. It is important to make note that in these instances, the use of the app is an opt-in experience; customers choose to use their mobile devices for a more convenient shopping experience. The use of store apps and mobile devices is not a necessary part of the shopping experience; it is simply offered as an added convenience.

Another alternative to integrating mobile devices into the shopping experience is requiring customers to use their mobile devices to shop a store. Amazon Go stores require shoppers to use their Amazon app to enter the store. They are then charged for purchases through the app as well. This frictionless shopping experience invites shoppers to spend as much or as little time in the store as schedules allow, as there are no sales associates, cash wraps, or lines to be blamed for a lengthy shopping trip.

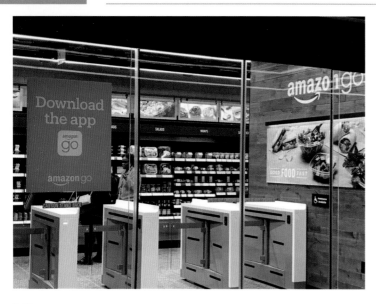

3.18
Amazon Go's shoppers are required to download and launch the Amazon or Amazon Go app in order to enter the store. The information included in the app, coupled with cameras and sensors throughout the store, create a frictionless shopping experience.

At Amazon Go stores, customers scan the Amazon Go (or Amazon) app on their mobile device to enter the store. Throughout their shopping experience, all they have to do is fill their shopping bag (backpack, purse, etc.) as they shop, then simply walk out the door when their shopping is complete. The concept of "Just Walk Out," a proprietary technology comprised of hundreds of cameras and sensors, is used at Amazon Go locations as customers are tracked through cameras and sensors throughout their time in the store; customers are only charged for items they leave the store with. Dubbed "legal shoplifting," the cost of their purchases is automatically charged to their Amazon account once they leave the store. Within minutes of walking out of an Amazon Go store, shoppers receive a notification outlining the total amount they have been charged, products purchased, and time spent in the store.

This proprietary technology is Amazon's solution for an oft-heard customer gripe: having to wait in line to checkout. As a result, the entire sales floor is dedicated to live product; there is no cash wrap.

The small store set-ups have allowed Amazon to test their cashier-less technology and in 2020, Amazon sold their proprietary platform to other retailers. Rather than relying on the Amazon app to enter the store, these retailers will require shoppers to insert a credit card into the turnstile to enter and begin their shopping. See the following Company Spotlight for more information about Amazon Go and their Just Walk Out technology.

Beacon technologies

Customers are bombarded with information through mobile devices, storefronts, and exterior signage, so retailers need to cut through the noise and send specific, targeted messages to customers. Retailers are utilizing beacon technologies to funnel targeted information directly to their customers. Retailers can push information to customers at any given moment. The benefit is that the messaging is sent to customers who have an interest in store events and activities; the user has downloaded the retailer's app and opted in to receive notifications. This directed messaging is targeting retailers' target customers.

Beacon technologies, first introduced by Apple in 2013, are tiny wireless devices (about the size of a sticker) that transmit signals that interact with the store's app. In order for the beacons to be utilized, shoppers must have installed the retailer's app *and* be in close proximity to the store; these signals show up as push notifications to the shopper. Beacons offer one-way communication between the retailer and consumer as retailers are able to send messages to customers but customers are not able to reply, ask questions, seek additional information, etc. The most widely used beacon technologies are based on location and are aptly named location-based services (LBS). Retailers use both outdoor and indoor location-based services.

The benefit to both retailers and customers is that beacon technologies are able to customize messages for users based on the user's profile, shopping history, and geographic location; this type of shopping experience can't be replicated solely through online shopping or the in-store experience. And as we know, modern shoppers are looking for customized experiences and personalized recommendations based on their shopping habits. Beacon technologies give retailers the opportunity to offer shoppers personalized discounts, rewards, and even recommendations sent directly to their customer's smartphones. It truly integrates the digital experience into the brick-and-mortar store as it utilizes the customer's smartphone to get them into the store and help them navigate throughout the store. Effective messaging can be directed at customers as they navigate through a store or while they are standing in front of a window. Beacon technologies alert apps or websites (that the user has opted into) when someone approaches or leaves a location; this drives increased user engagement.

Outdoor location-based (or proximity-based) services connect retailers and customers based on where customers are at any given moment; this means that customers are notified about events, sales, promotions, etc. during both intentional and unintentional shopping trips, encouraging them to pop into a store because of push notifications. These geolocation services utilize a smartphone's GPS to match shoppers' whereabouts to local businesses and special offers. This means that retailers know when their best customers are nearby and can reach out and invite them into its stores with a message or promotional offer. LBS are a great way to "remind" existing customers to visit the store. LBS technologies, in their simplest form, provide the ability to track someone's exact location through his or her mobile device. In general, LBS allows retailers to "find" customers when they come near the stores and to deliver a targeted sales message, usually in the form of a text message. In general, customers engage retail LBS via a mobile app such as Foursquare or Shopkick. Customers download the app and then access all of the data and benefits through the app's interface. Foursquare created a rewards program to recognize its most avid users, so there is an added benefit to using the app.

Beacon technologies are also beneficial when customers are already in a store as these technologies not only reach shoppers where they are (glued to their phones!), but can also help shoppers navigate around the store. **Indoor location-based services** allow the same kind of tracking and promotional capabilities as outdoor LBS, but target customers who are already inside a store. Rather than using LBS to entice customers to wander into the store, this type of location-based service works to *keep* customers in a store. Once inside a retail location, it can remind them to visit other departments, direct them to store events, or encourage them to buy more to receive additional rewards. Beacon technologies can direct customers to the exact aisle, department, or in-store location to find the product they are seeking. Beacons can replace the sometimes hard-to-find sales associate, alleviating customer frustrations by allowing customers to be directed to what they were looking for rather than aimlessly wandering throughout the store. This technology is based on Bluetooth beacons throughout the store that connect to mobile devices. This is especially beneficial in large stores or malls like Macy's or Mall of America as customers are alerted about deals and items they may be interested in. This kind of precision marketing can be very effective. It uses real-time data based on consumer behavior to deliver immediate, personalized content and initiate ongoing communication with shoppers to drive loyalty and sales. The beacons push notifications to users as they walk around the store.

Company Spotlight:
The future of shopping: Amazon Go

This is why Amazon is calling it the "Just Walk Out" shopping experience: no line to wait in, no one rifling through bags to count the number of items purchased, no scanning and no need to check in with an employee.

What is your biggest pain point when shopping brick-and-mortar? If standing and waiting in line is one of your gripes, you are not alone; 60 percent of US shoppers say that waiting in line is their number one in-store frustration (Retail Info Systems, 2017). How can retailers address this? Leave it to Amazon to offer a solution!

Amazon, best known for their online shopping experience, is no longer just an e-commerce site. The tech behemoth has been rolling out cashier-less convenient stores in some of the biggest cities in the world, introducing their "grab and go" technology as a solution to requiring customers to wait in line to complete their purchase.

First piloted in Seattle in 2016 to Amazon employees, additional stores opened in Seattle, San Francisco, Chicago, New York, and London; the list continues to grow. What began as a slow rollout is expected to pick up speed as Amazon is reportedly looking to open 3,000 Amazon Go stores by 2021.

How does it work? How is a cashier-less store different than self-check kiosks seen at the likes of Target and Wal-Mart? The Amazon Go experience truly is "grab and go"; there is no line or checkout process. The shopping experience is all monitored via computer vision, sensor fusion, and deep machine learning throughout one's time spent in-store. Customers are tracked as icons as they navigate the store. Store shelves are weighted, so when products are picked up or moved, Amazon Go employees are instantly notified and the product is either restocked or product placement is adjusted.

Let's back up. . . what does all this mean and how does Amazon Go actually work? It all starts with the Amazon app. Shoppers use the Amazon (or Amazon Go) app on their mobile device in order to enter the store. As customers approach the store, they will see turnstiles signifying they should launch the app in order to scan the Amazon Go QR code. This activates the turnstiles to allow

3.19
Customers are reminded of the ease and convenience of shopping frictionless retail at Amazon Go stores. Their "Just Walk Out Shopping" approach allows shoppers to complete their shopping and then simply walk out of the store as payment is made through credit and/or debit cards linked the shopper's Amazon account. Customers do not need to be rung up, scan their merchandise, or check in with a sales associate.

customers to enter. From that point on, phones can be put away so hands are free for shopping.

Once inside the store, shoppers are free to roam around the stores, ranging from 1,200–2,300 square feet. Customers are invited to grab products throughout their shopping excursion, whether or not they end up purchasing said items. Should customers change their mind about products, they can simply set them back down on store shelves. Upon deciding to make a purchase, shoppers may carry the product around in their hands or products can be dropped into their shopping bag, backpack, or handbag. When their shopping experience is complete, the customer simply walks out the door. This is exactly why Amazon is calling it the "Just Walk Out" shopping experience: no line to wait in, no one rifling through bags to count the number of items purchased, no scanning and no need to check in with an employee. Shoppers grab their merchandise and head out.

The entire shopping experience has been tracked and monitored through a combination of artificial intelligence, computer vision, and data pulled from sensors to ensure customers are only charged for what they leave with. When the shopping excursion is complete, shoppers receive a push notification outlining time spent in the store, amount spent, and products purchased.

What about shoppers who don't have a smartphone, Amazon account, or the Amazon (or Amazon Go) app? Amazon continues to evolve this frictionless shopping experience to ensure all customers have access to the store:

- Shoppers can buddy up! Shoppers can enter and shop alongside friends who have scanned them in, which means their friends will also be footing the bill for the purchases.
- For shoppers who don't have the Amazon app, they can scan an Amazon QR code (found on the turnstile) that will direct them to create an Amazon account.
- Amazon Go employees can scan customers in. These customers will then complete any purchases manually with an Amazon Go employee.

The small store set-ups have allowed Amazon to test their Just Walk Out technology; the cashier-less checkout system was well received. In 2020, Amazon sold their proprietary platform to other retailers. In 2020, airport retailer CIBO Express Gourmet Market opened two stores that utilize Amazon's Just Walk Out technology. At these locations, rather than customers scanning the Amazon app, they will enter the store by scanning their credit card. Their credit card will then be charged for the items they leave the store with.

Download the Amazon or Amazon Go app.

Open the app and scan the QR code.

Walk thorugh the turnstile to begin your shopping.

Grab what you need and drop it into your shopping bag, backpack, or handbag

Just walk out; no need to scan the items. Your Amazon account will be automatically charged.

Amazon will send you a receipt outlining your visit and products purchased.

3.20
Here is how it works
Images by Cody Banks

The integration of beacon technology in the retail environment allows brick-and-mortar retailers to capture today's shopper (who is oftentimes glued to their phone). It offers a new way to engage with consumers, provide incentives for shoppers to enter a store, take their time looking around, and hopefully not leave empty-handed.

Are customized push notifications effective? Think about the last time you shopped online; based on the products you looked at and/or placed in your shopping cart, did you receive other product suggestions from the retailer? It is likely that you did; these recommendations are carefully calculated using algorithms. These algorithms take into account browsing and shopping history to make product suggestions accordingly. Retailers use algorithms as a suggestive selling tool; these are highly effective as the online retailer has learned about your preferences. Now, imagine you receive specific and relevant product suggestions right to your phone when you are in the immediate area to make a purchase. Sounds tempting, right? You are not alone!

A 2014 study found that over 70 percent of shoppers who received beacon-triggered push notifications on their smartphone said it increased their likelihood to make a purchase during a store visit. More than 60 percent of respondents said they'd do more holiday shopping at brick-and-mortar stores that delivered mobile content and offers while they shopped, and 61 percent of people said they'd simply visit a store more often if they offered beacon marketing campaigns (da Silva, 2017). Attractive numbers from a business perspective!

So what does all this mean? When customers are in close proximity to a retailer whose app they have downloaded and the retailer utilizes beacons, customers will receive push notifications letting them know about special events, sales, and promotions that are going on in-store. These notifications will be relevant to the user based on their search history or shopping habits. These shoppers may not have intended to visit the store, but given the push notifications they received, the retailer has incentivized the customer to amend their initial plans and make a trip *into* the store.

In 2014, Macy's rolled out, what was, at that time, retail's largest beacon installation. Macy's installed 4,000 beacons to engage shoppers as they entered Macy's stores. Customers who had the Macy's app were reminded to open their Macy's app to receive notifications, promotions, deals, and discount offerings. After some successful testing at their New York City and San Francisco flagship stores, Macy's implemented the use of beacon technology in all of its stores nationwide.

How do shoppers know if retailers use beacon technologies? Well, visually, there is no indication. Beacons are tiny, and virtually invisible to the eye. But, grab your phone and head over to your favorite store and the message becomes quite clear. If you begin to receive push notifications through the retailer's app as you near the store's location, you know they are using beacon technologies to connect with shoppers.

Quick Response (QR) codes

In the early 2000's, **QR codes** were introduced to the marketplace, primarily as a marketing tool that led users to brand websites. However, it was not a streamlined process with the corresponding smartphone technology as users were required to first download an app to read the QR code. There were simply too many steps in order to effectively use the QR codes. For this reason, QR codes, once thought of as "the way of the future," disappeared. Fast-forward to where we are today, and QR codes have re-emerged. They are much more compatible with the current technology in smartphones as no additional apps are needed to access information from the QR code. Retailers have taken note.

3.21
An employee scans the quick response (QR) code of a handbag at the Reebonz Pte headquarters in Singapore. Singapore-based Reebonz, Southeast Asia's biggest luxury e-commerce company, sells bags, shoes, and jewelry by brands including Givenchy, Chanel, and Christian Louboutin using a flash sales model, which offers limited-time deals at steep discounts.

Not only have smartphones changed since the early 2000s, but consumer behavior has as well. Smartphones are engrained in just about every part of our lives. As a result, retailers are integrating QR codes within the retail environment. The primary use of QR codes within brick-and-mortar stores is information gathering. QR codes can inform and educate shoppers on products and price points as well as help customers efficiently navigate stores to track down merchandise.

To eliminate the feeling that shopping is like a scavenger hunt, the Nike House of Innovation 000 uses QR codes on mannequins to direct customers to product within the store. Shoppers use the Nike app to scan QR codes that are featured alongside mannequins. Information is immediately available about what the mannequin is dressed in, in-store availability, and sizing. This eliminates the need to seek out sales associates for merchandise, sizes, and product information, creating a more convenient shopping experience.

QR codes have also become an important part of WeChat for payment purposes. QR codes can be used by either the retailer or the customer to complete their purchase. If used by the retailer, in order to checkout, they will scan the customer's WeChat barcode or QR code, payment is immediately transferred to complete the purchase. The other option is for the customer to scan the retailer's QR code and follow the prompts to complete the purchase.

Company Spotlight: FIT:MATCH

FIT:MATCH uses revolutionary neuro network matching technology to show customers apparel items that fit them 90% or better; and simply hides the rest.

In Chapter 1, we introduced the idea of a retail store without any merchandise, as seen with Nordstrom Local stores. A variation of a store without merchandise is a fashion retailer selling apparel and accessories, yet there is no apparel or accessory items to be seen. Instead, the sales floor is a series of digital screens inviting shoppers to interact and engage. Meet FIT:MATCH, the integrated online–offline AI-powered apparel shopping match platform.

FIT: MATCH was created as a shopping platform to combat fit risk, or concerns and uncertainties customers feel when making a purchase without trying on the products (which results in high return rates and inventory forecasting inaccuracies).

FIT:MATCH partners with apparel brands to increase accessibility while taking the guesswork out of shopping and eliminating fit risk. FIT:MATCH uses revolutionary neuro network matching technology to show customers apparel items that fit them 90% or better; and simply hides the rest. The company's systems recommend apparel products based on the customer's fit and style preferences, specs of the apparel garments, and accurate biometric data of the shoppers. Product recommendations are personalized for each customer, leading to improved retail economics: higher conversions and fewer product returns.

The FIT:MATCH studio locations appear to be void of live merchandise; when shoppers enter the brick-and-mortar locations or kiosks, they are face-to-face with digital screens rather than fixtures and shelves merchandised with the anticipated shirts, pants, sweaters, etc. they may be shopping for.

How does it work?
Inside the physical space, 3D-AI software is used to collect over 150-sub-centimeter-accurate body measurements in a matter of 10 seconds

(users are "fitched"). Shoppers complete a fit and style profile questionnaire, allowing the software program to better understand customer preferences in terms of fit, brand assortment, personal aesthetic, and lifestyle.

Once the 3D-AI measurements are taken and the registration process is complete, shoppers log into their favorite partner brand's website to access their top matches. With the click of a button, they are able to purchase product recommendations with confidence. Shoppers also receive personalized text and email messages with their top matches each week.

FIT:MATCH's first interactive retail space opened in Baybrook Mall in Houston, Texas,

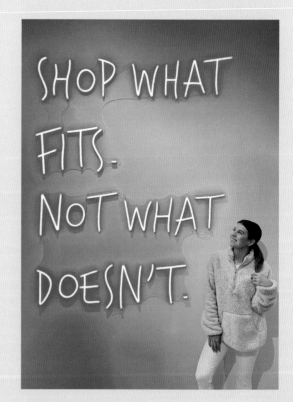

3.22

3.23 and 3.24
Shoppers utilize the in-store technology to shop products that will fit their body shape.

during the holiday 2019 season. The initial launch was well received. Because the shopping experience is so different from what we are used to, there is a learning curve involved. However, FIT:MATCH created an easy-to-use program; as a result, consumers responded favorably. Some 80 percent of people who came into the FIT:MATCH Studio (the vast majority who were just passersby and had no idea about the concept) enthusiastically participated in the experience on the promise of never having to try on clothes again. Eighty-six percent of participants reported

either loving or liking the experience; 71 percent of participants reported that they pretty quickly understood the concept and process based on the instructions provided by the store staff. The remaining 29 percent said they understood it; no one said they did not get it.

FIT:MATCH imagines a world where everyone shops with a Fitch credential, always from their own AI-matched assortment, never having to try on clothes or deal with fit-related returns again. FIT:MATCH has plans to expand throughout the United States in the second half of 2020.

Virtual shopping bag

The Nike House of Innovation 000 uses the app's virtual shopping bag to fill physical dressing rooms for customers. Within the Nike app, shoppers add items to a virtual try-on list, which is then added to a virtual bag; when the bag is full (aka the customer is done shopping and ready to try on), the Nike team is notified. Products from the virtual bag are pulled from the sales floor and/or stockroom and sent to a fitting room. The room, and desired products, are ready and waiting when the customer arrives. The customer has free hands throughout the shopping excursion so they are able to engage with the Nike brand through multiple touchpoints; they are not weighted down carrying merchandise throughout the store, balancing product, technology, and personal belongings.

How does this impact visual merchandising teams?

Visual merchandisers are responsible for brand communication. Visual merchandisers make information readily available for consumers throughout their shopping experience. However, customers shop differently! Not all customers are seeking the same information. For example, 63 percent of male shoppers use their mobile devices for price checking products before making a purchase, whereas 48 percent of women use their smartphones to download digital coupons while shopping.

This makes the job of a visual merchandiser especially challenging because they must strike a balance between too much signage and not enough. Too much signage and customers stop reading; not enough signage, and customers become frustrated and head for the closest exit sign.

Summary

Omnichannel retail provides shoppers with an enhanced shopping experience, integrating multiple touchpoints to connect with shoppers and close the sale when and where it is most convenient for customers. There is much overlap between the virtual and physical shopping experiences as shoppers are using mobile devices in brick-and-mortar stores and in-store shoppers are directed to digital platforms for increased engagement. Branded apps, connected retailers, tablets, and social media sites are just a few ways retailers are engaging shoppers and enticing them to not only make a purchase, but also connect with the brand for increased brand loyalty.

> **KEY TERMS**
>
> **Beacon technologies**
> **Brand-generated content**
> **Endless aisles**
> **Indoor location-based services**
> **Machine learning**
> **QR code**
> **User-generated content**

CRITICAL THINKING: THE APPLICATION PROCESS

After completing the chapter readings, reflect on the information and experiences shared. Apply what you learned to future retail experiences:

1. The chapter calls attention to examples of how digital technologies are integrated in brick-and-mortar stores; what others should be included?
2. Think about pain points you have experienced while shopping; how can these be addressed through digital technologies? What innovative ideas do you have to shape the evolution of retail?
3. Amazon Go store locations are found in busy, urban areas for on-the-go customers. They are now selling their proprietary technology to other retailers, such as airport retailer CIBO Express. What other retailers and/or locations would benefit from this "Just Walk Out" technology?
4. How might retailers create awareness of events, promotions, and/or store proximity to customers who don't have the retailer's app?
5. TikTok is growing in popularity; propose one in-store, branded social media moment based on TikTok challenges.

4

Store planning and design

Overview

Throughout the text we have addressed the challenges retailers face in simply getting customers to walk through their doors, so as you can imagine, once they are in the store, retailers work hard to keep customers in the store as long as possible. Effective utilization of space, through floor plans and space management, create a shoppable environment. Additionally, brands and retailers need to consider interior elements such as fixtures, lighting, and use of mannequins; this is where store planning comes in.

4.1
The store design of the Uniqlo mega shop at Tokyo's Shinjuku district dictates product placement as permanent built-ins wrap around the store walls.

What is store planning?

Store planning and design is an important component of visual merchandising. Visual merchandising focuses on the display of products whereas in **store planning**, the focus is on the physical space. Store planning and design include space allocation, store layout, floor and wall coverings, and fixture types; these elements work together to maximize sales per square foot. However, because of the changing demands of shoppers, the brick-and-mortar retail environment is changing as well; the likes of experiential retail, showrooming, and pop-up shops are just a few ways the physical retail environment has shifted.

Retailers are allocating dedicated floor space to the customer experience, rather than merchandising and product display.

Brick-and-mortar stores are taking on the role of a showroom, offering shoppers the opportunity to touch, feel, and try products on before completing the purchase online. Pop-up shops allow retailers to be more nimble in their physical store presence as these are not permanent storefronts. These are considerations that store planning teams must keep in mind as they work to create dynamic brick-and-mortar stores.

An important starting point is the store layout; store layout creates a space that shoppers can easily navigate, find product, and complete their purchase in a convenient, hassle-free manner.

As a shopper, the store layout seems fairly basic: four walls, retail fixtures, a cash wrap (maybe!), shelves, and mannequin displays.

4.2
Primark's largest flagship store in Madrid, Spain, on Gran Via, is thoughtfully designed both in function and aesthetic.

Not too difficult, right? If only it were that easy! The overall design of a retail store can literally make or break the retail business. An ineffective, confusing, or uninviting space will have shoppers running for the nearest exit as fast as possible. So what are additional considerations for store planning teams? This is not an exhaustive list, but some initial considerations for store planning teams:

- How many floors will the store be?
- Will there be aisles in the store? How wide will the aisles be in terms of customer movement?
- Will the fixtures be custom or standard?
- What type of mannequins and/or dress forms will feature apparel or accessory items?
- What type of lighting will be used?
- Will there be anything other than store fixtures on the sales floor? (i.e., seating area, kids play area, tech hub, etc.)
- What type, if any, in-store experiences will be used?
- What is the overall brand aesthetic? How will the brick-and-mortar environment support this aesthetic?

These are just a few ideas of components that must be considered by store planning teams. Next time you are out shopping, really analyze the store environment. Remember that everything you see has been strategically placed there for a reason; nothing is coincidental. Why do you think store planning teams made that decision?

Store layouts are the foundation that will guide the shopping experience within the retail space that will (hopefully) help move merchandise and create an enjoyable shopping experience for customers.

Today's shoppers are educated consumers; they enter stores armed with knowledge: product knowledge, price, customer reviews, comparable products, etc.; they don't need to be sold on products. They do, however, expect to be able to quickly and efficiently find the products they are looking for.

According to Paco Underhill, founder of Envirosell and author of *Why We Buy: The Science of Shopping*, the interior retail store layout has two important components:

- **Store Design:** This includes strategic floor plans and space management, including furniture, displays, fixtures, lighting, and signage.
- **Customer Flow:** The pattern of behavior and way in which a customer navigates through a store. Understanding customer flow and identifying common patterns that emerge as customers navigate through a store. The way in which customers interact with merchandise based on the store layout is critical for retail merchandising strategies. Physical retailers are able to track this using analytics software and data from in-store video and the Wi-Fi signal from smartphones.

These two components work in tandem to create an enjoyable and efficient shopping experience.

"Effective store design is an essential building block in garnering strong relationships with customers. Design touches every aspect of the retail experience. It narrates the brand and product story, it educates customers, it inspires and entertains, and it leads customers to make a purchase. Retailers that place a high importance on design innovation are the ones that will thrive." Walter Miranda, Harbor Retail, CEO

What to expect: store interiors

Did you know that 90 percent of shoppers turn right when they walk into a store? (Orvis, 2017) What does that mean for store planning?

Store planning is the foundational step in creating the ideal retail environment, as architects and store design teams think strategically about how to best utilize square footage to not only sell product, but to positively impact the overall branded customer experience. A customers' ability to interact with store merchandise affects their buying behavior: accessibility and product engagement increases purchases. Accessibility starts with the interior layout of the store itself. Store planning teams oftentimes have a background in architecture or interior design to better understand the store's physical structure.

A store's layout should subtly guide customers through the store, exposing them to sellable merchandise, while simultaneously keeping them engaged in the shopping experience in order to inspire them to make a purchase. If shoppers are continually drawn to the next fixture, display, or in-store experience, the retailer has successfully created an enjoyable and efficient shopping experience. The shopping experience is not forced, challenging, or frustrating; store product, information, and in-store experiences are well merchandised and easily accessible.

An important aspect of the in-store experience is cohesive branding. The entire shopping experience should reinforce the brand's message. A shopper's first impression is the store exterior, but as soon as they pass

4.3
Diesel store on Bond Street in London.

4.4
Saks Fifth Avenue uses a mannequin grouping to welcome shoppers to the store. This transition area allows customers to ease their way into the store as they are subtly introduced to a seasonal theme and product recommendations as highlighted by "Saks It List."

through the front doors, the overall brand aesthetic should be cohesive. From color to font to fixture choices, the store interior and exterior should be consistent; branded messaging from digital and printed marketing materials should be integrated throughout the store.

Oftentimes when we enter a retail store, we are not inundated with product immediately; the retailer is giving customers time to get acclimated to the store. This is called the **transition area** or decompression zone. As shoppers enter a store, they are looking around to familiarize themselves with the space, determining where they need to go and how to best navigate the store; they are transitioning from exterior to interior. As a result, any product placed within this transition zone (typically 5–15 feet) is overlooked; for this reason, retailers refrain from featuring important signage and/or merchandise in the transition zone.

So what might be found in the transition area? Well, surprisingly, little to nothing. This should be an open space where customers

transition from one environment to the next. They are familiarizing themselves with the store, layout, and merchandise; they are not quite ready to begin the decision-making process. Therefore, retailers have adjusted their merchandising strategies to reduce and/or eliminate product from the transition area to avoid missed opportunities. The transition area introduces shoppers to the store environment and sets the tone for the shopping experience. This is accomplished through visual design elements such as wall and floor coverings, lighting, music, and signage.

Once shoppers have entered the store and are settled in the store environment, they are ready to navigate through the store and (hopefully!) spend their hard-earned money.

Because majority of customers veer to the right upon entering a store, products placed on the right side of the store receive immediate attention; retailers use this space to create a strong first impression. On-trend product, compelling merchandise displays, and interactive experiences capture the attention of shoppers and entice them to continue exploring throughout the store.

There are really five primary store layouts you will find used most often by retailers:

1. Grid
2. Herringbone
3. Loop (Racetrack)
4. Free-flow
5. Forced path

Grid

The grid configuration is most commonly used at convenience stores and grocery stores, offering customers long aisles of merchandise to shop from. The focus is on function as the grid layout emphasizes the products that are for sale. Retailers are able to target customers through promotions, as the traffic flow is predictable; shoppers weave up and down the aisles in a methodical way.

Because traffic flow is predictable, retailers are able to use targeted promotions on endcaps. (Endcaps are product displays, typically shelves, placed at the end of aisles. Endcaps are highly visible and garner a lot of attention from shoppers, giving a competitive advantage.) However, the somewhat forced traffic flow can be frustrating for shoppers as it is difficult to find shortcuts when navigating the store.

Herringbone

The herringbone configuration is similar to the grid layout but is a better fit for narrow stores. The aisles are shorter in length and can feel cramped for shoppers. To add visual appeal, there is oftentimes a display (be it a promotional item or seating group) at the end of some of the rows. Your local library likely uses the herringbone layout.

Loop

The loop configuration is oftentimes referred to as a racetrack as it subtly leads shoppers around a closed loop. This loop layout provides a predictable traffic flow as it strategically guides shoppers past all the merchandise in the store from store entrance right up to the checkout. If executed well, the loop layout ensures product promotions are highly visible because of the controlled traffic flow. Additionally, retailers are able to tell a methodical story to shoppers, as they know the exact path shoppers are taking as they navigate the store.

Free-flow

The free-flow layout is exactly what it sounds like: there is no one configuration in which shoppers are ushered through the store. There is no predictable traffic pattern as shoppers are encouraged to explore the store merchandise in their own methodical way. Store planning and design teams can be creative in their merchandising strategies based on inventory levels, product offerings, and square footage. This layout is typically used by upscale retailers who have limited merchandise and inventory levels.

The free-form configuration can result in a confusing and frustrating shopping experience, as there are no directives to guide shoppers throughout the space. The store layout is unfamiliar so customers don't know where to find merchandise and/or product categories. However, the free-flow configuration provides more flexibility for retailers to adapt to changing trends both in product offerings and within the retail industry. For example, as we see an increase in in-store experiences, retailers using the free-flow layout can incorporate experiential retail much easier than some of the other retail configurations.

Forced path

IKEA is a great example of a retailer that uses a forced path layout. In this configuration, the retailer uses walls, doors, and fixtures to create a pre-determined route shoppers will take. The benefit of using a forced path layout is that retailers know exactly how customers will navigate through the store. As a result, shoppers are exposed to an increased amount of merchandise because they have been directed to follow a specific path throughout the store. The disadvantage of a forced path layout is that customers can become frustrated that they cannot move throughout the store quickly and efficiently.

4.5
The Balenciaga store in London. What store layout is this considered to be?

4.6
At the Uniqlo outlet, product is highly visible at the end of each row, directing shoppers to product that can be found as they explore each aisle. Fast Retailing expects their Ginza Uniqlo outlet to be the biggest revenue generator in their network.

Are retailers limited to just one type of layout? Absolutely not! Larger stores like Nordstrom that have various departments at different price points incorporate different layouts. Nordstrom uses different in-store configurations to differentiate between departments and price points. Other retailers, like Target, use the loop layout and the grid layout simultaneously. In many Target locations, a loop layout is what shoppers initially see and experience, but in the middle of the loop, fixtures are placed in a grid configuration.

Another important component of store planning and design is understanding the merchandise categories and inventory levels carried by the retailer. This affects fixture quantity, type, and placement on the sales floor. The sales floor should always appear to be full and "of the now," meaning on-trend merchandise should be highly visible to the target customer. During different times of the year there are different inventory levels, and the sales floor will reflect these variances. As we all know, the fourth quarter (which includes holiday) in retail is the busiest time of the year and inventory levels are highest. This means that high capacity fixtures should be on the sales floor to maximize the number of units on the floor. However, once the fourth quarter wraps up, sales slow and inventory levels decrease. The high capacity fixtures should be swapped out with smaller fixtures to accommodate lower inventory levels. If the high capacity fixtures were left on the floor, the sales floor would appear empty, giving the impression that the store is going out of business. This is not a good look for retailers! Lower capacity fixtures will ensure that the sales floor still looks full, and in turn, gives the impression that the business is thriving.

Company Spotlight:
Harbor Retail

Harmonic Retail™ eliminates the different retail channels (online and offline), inviting the retailer to operate as one, rather than two channels.

Harbor Retail is a retail-design company that integrates physical design with digital engagements for today's shoppers. They create retail environments that are integrated, immersive, and on-brand in order to drive memorable customer experiences. Harbor works with brands on strategy and planning for brick-and-mortar spaces, the overall retail design, integration of retail technologies, custom fixtures, and store logistics. They are a one-stop shop for all parts of the design and build process. It is no wonder they have moved beyond omnichannel retail and are focusing on what they have trademarked as "harmonic retail." Harbor Retail = Harmonic Retail™.

What does that mean?
Harbor Retail describes Harmonic Retail™ as "a shift beyond converged commerce where online and offline experiences don't merely integrate, but they interact, enrich and react upon one another to create a living, harmonized brand expression throughout the customer journey."

Harmonic Retail™ eliminates the different retail channels (online and offline), inviting the retailer to operate as one, rather than two channels. Ecommerce is the foundation of Harmonic Retail™, rather than brick-and-mortar; from there, the additional branded touchpoints (apps, email, social media, print, events, etc.) support the e-commerce experience.

Have you seen their work?
If you shop the likes of Nordstrom, West Elm, and Starbucks, you have experienced Harbor's Harmonic Retail™. They seamlessly blend the physical and digital store experiences to anticipate customer's needs, creating lifetime customer value.

Harbor Retail's store-within-a-store for Samsung, CHEF COLLECTION & Family Hub: Experiential path-to-purchase, custom build and digital engagement IoT experience design featuring Harbor's Self Healing Technology™

www.HarborRetail.com   HARBOR

4.7
Harbor Retail's store-within-a-store for Samsung, CHEF COLLECTION & Family Hub: Experiential path-to-purchase, customer build and digital engagement IoT experience design featuring Harbor's Self Healing Technology™.

Square footage vs. selling space

The square footage of a store is not the same as the store's selling space. This is an important consideration for retailers in order to plan for inventory levels and maximize sales. **Square footage** is a measurement of a two-dimensional space, or, for a retailer, the overall size of the store.

Selling space, however, is the amount of space on the floor that is dedicated to displaying product. The areas of the floor where there are fixtures, tables, and seating arrangements are considered selling space. However, areas like stock rooms and washrooms are part of the store's square footage, but not selling space.

In recent years, retailers have recognized that the sales floor should include more than just fixtures and inventory. In today's retail environment, sales floors include accessible product, seating areas, and in-store experiences, ranging from physical to digital experiences.

As we have discussed throughout the text, social media interactions and experiences have become expectations in the retail environment. Shoppers seek out these experiences to not only learn about the brands, but also to share experiences with their networks. Retailers are utilizing social media moments to engage shoppers, creating brand awareness and long term customers.

This means dedicating valuable selling space to these social media experiences. Most store budgets are based on sales per square foot, so removing fixtures and sellable merchandise from the selling floor can be worrisome. (Sales per square foot gauges how efficient a retailer is using their space; it is measured by looking at sales figures and the store square footage.) However, customer's expectations are changing, so retailers must adapt as well.

As retailers gauge their successes based off of sales per square foot, there is not an immediate metric to determine the value these social media experiences add to the bottom line of the store. Oftentimes the social media interactions result in future sales, rather than immediate sales. Retailers may look to measure social media interactions, such as increased followers, likes, check-ins, and tagging to gauge customer interest in in-store social media experiences.

In addition to social media moments and in-store experiences, retailers are also dedicating square footage to include charging stations on the sales floor. In the past, retailers have included accessible outlets for shoppers to plug in their mobile devices to charge while they shop, but now, access to one's mobile device has become increasingly important as

4.8
Lengermann & Trieschmann (L&T), a sports and fashion house in Germany, dedicates ample square footage to create an in-store experience for customers. It is standing room only as customers take time away from shopping to watch a football game.

shoppers are becoming more reliant on these devices. Not only are shoppers utilizing mobile devices to research products, seek advice, complete their purchase, and share purchases with their social networks, but retailers are creating in-store experiences that seek customer engagement through mobile devices. To ensure that customers have the opportunity to fully engage with the in-store digital experience, retailers are now incorporating secure charging stations throughout the store.

Not only does this service help keep customers in the store longer (the longer they shop, the more their device will be charged!), but it could also incentivize passersby to stop in and charge their phone, resulting in time spent looking at the retailer's product offerings.

Secure charging stations allow shoppers to explore the store while their device is securely locked, eliminating the need for shoppers to simply plug in their phone and remain in one place while it charges. Instead, as their phone charges, shoppers are able to wander throughout the store, increasing exposure to products and services offered by the retailer, and, in turn, increasing the likelihood of making a purchase.

The charging stations take up little space on the sale floor, but placement is important so that it is accessible to customers but does not impede the shopping experience. Store planning teams need to be conscious of how services like charging stations are used. For example, charging stations should be situated along the perimeter of the store as to not block entry points, aisles, or fixtures, creating a bottleneck for customers. There also needs to be considerable space around the charging station to allow for customers to situate themselves both before and after using

4.9
Another addition to the sales floor we are seeing is the inclusion of charging stations. Charging stations, as seen at Nordstrom's Toronto Eaton Centre and Under Armour, enable shoppers to securely charge their mobile devices while they shop. This ultimately keeps customers in the store longer, resulting in increased sales.

the charging station. The charging stations provide added conveniences for shoppers, but if placed improperly on the sales floor, they can also create real inconveniences for customers.

Retailers need to prioritize their integration of technologies into the brick-and-mortar shopping experience. It is imperative that retailers are cognizant of their target market and their target customer's reliance on digital technologies.

HRC Retail Advisory is a retail strategic advisory firm that helps retailers navigate, adapt and compete in a rapidly transforming retail marketplace. According to an April 2018 consumer survey from HRC, here are some interesting findings as it pertains to the integration of digital technologies in the brick-and-mortar retail environment:

Store Environment
- Eighty-five percent said the store environment is an important feature when shopping.

Customer Service
- Ninety-five percent of shoppers want to be left alone when shopping.

In-Store Tech Offerings
- In-store tech offerings that fulfill customer service needs (price scanner, apps that provide promotional information) are much more important to shoppers than dressing room tech, mobile payment, and in-store events.
- Thirty percent of respondents ranked free in-store Wi-Fi as an important store feature (the rate was much higher among younger shoppers who rely more heavily on their social networks while they shop).
- Seventeen percent identified dressing room technology that assists in shopping to be important.
- Thirty-seven percent think tech-enhanced dressing rooms are important in clothing stores.
- Six percent ranked customized lighting in dressing rooms to be important.

Omnichannel
- Sixty-five percent of shoppers said that the "buy online, pick up in-store" option is important when buying apparel.
- Forty-two percent of Millennial and 38 percent of Gen Z respondents identified "reserve online and try on in-store" as important elements for apparel purchases.

Apps
- Thirty-four percent ranked receiving promotional and sales information directly via smartphone when entering a store important.
- Seventy-six percent rated an in-store app that provides personal recommendations as important.
- Eight percent wanted the option to pay via a mobile app.

Social Media
- Nearly 70 percent of Gen Z and 63 percent of Millennials use social media to share pictures and gather opinions from friends and family before they buy
- Nineteen percent said special events to create a sense of community were important (24 percent of Gen Zers).

Mobile Pay
- Thirty percent said the ability to pay a sales associate from anywhere in the store is important.

Multi-store retailers: Creating cohesive spaces

Ever wonder how multi-store retailers ensure consistent and cohesive visual displays and store layouts in multiple locations? Although the physical structure and square footage vary from one location to the next, the overall brand aesthetic is clear. Fixtures, merchandise placement, store layout, interior and exterior displays, fitting rooms. . . regardless of the store location, the store itself always feels familiar. Although it may be your first time in that particular store location, it feels no different than the other locations you have shopped before. How is this accomplished?

Some retailers (let's be honest. . . those with large budgets!) have physical mock-up spaces where they merchandise product and install displays on a smaller scale to assess both the function and aesthetic of the store layout and merchandising. Typically, these mock-up spaces are housed within the corporate offices for easy access to integrate sample product and fixtures into the space. This gives merchandisers, buyers, and store design teams the opportunity to meet on-site to merchandise the mock-up space, assess product placement, assign fixtures, and tweak the seasonal buy in order to create a compelling sales floor. They are able to see how product works to complement each other and encourage add-on sales as well as experience first-hand how customers navigate throughout the store. Once the design and merchandising is fully executed in the mock-up space, photos are taken and distributed to each store as a guide for their installation of the new season's product. Tweaks are made at the store-level based on square footage, inventory levels, and display accessibility.

However, as new technologies are introduced, these physical spaces are no longer a necessary way for retailers to test out store layouts; there are virtual resources to create, evaluate, and refine plans for their physical spaces. Software programs and virtual reality technology allow retailers, brands, and manufacturers to build realistic, accurate digital store layouts to test customer flow, planograms, and product placement.

4.10
An on-site showroom at corporate offices enables merchandising, store planning, buying, and marketing teams the opportunity to collaborate on optimizing the sales floor for the best customer experience.

Digital resources: Software programs and CAD programs

More and more retailers work off of digitally rendered corporate directives that outline seasonal themes and trends, fixtures, signage, and display guidelines. Corporate directives ensure that stores company-wide have the same expectations for overall visual aesthetic, but these renderings are created using computer-aided design (CAD) programs.

Merchandising and store design teams are able to work more efficiently both in planning and communication as these programs are cloud-based, allowing users to work in real time to review, edit, and make recommendations.

There is an array of programs that allow merchandising and store planning teams to work more efficiently; it is important to remember that retailers and corresponding departments have different needs, and therefore, use different programs. The overall size and scale of a company as well as the size and scale of the physical retail footprint affect the type of programs used.

Our purpose here is to introduce you to some of the industry's leaders in digital communication.

MockShop

MockShop, part of Visual Retailing, allows retailers to create virtual 3D mockups of their store. To ensure the entire look and feel of the virtual store is accurate, users can input store-specific fixtures and inventory. Retailers are able to create planograms and visual guidelines for stores to follow, ensuring consistency across markets. The MockShop software saves time and money, allowing planograms and visual directives to be more focused and detailed for each store location, improving brand awareness.

How is MockShop used by store planning teams? MockShop provides users the ability to create true-to-space floor plans and planograms; brands and retailers are able to upload actual product and fixtures for floor sets and seasonal buys and place them on the sales floor. This ensures that planogram truly reflects what the physical retail sales floor will look like. Fixtures and product can be moved around through the virtual floorplan, allowing retailers to evaluate and assess product placement and traffic flow. Upon final review, the recommended floor plan and merchandising strategies can be distributed company-wide for brand consistency.

Visual Retailing is comprised of four different elements used by different divisions of retailers. You can learn more about MockShop and Visual Retailing in the Company Spotlight.

Retail Smart

Retail Smart offers retail planning solutions to optimize space within brick-and-mortar stores. Their team of retail planning experts address how each product contributes to store profits and then makes recommendations for store layout and merchandising strategies to increase sales and maximize profits.

Retailers can also utilize the Retail Smart software to create planograms and evaluate merchandising strategies. The software breaks down the sales floor by category and department, helping retailers to understand how their profits are allocated according to product placement. After analyzing sales by category, merchandise can be redistributed throughout the sales floor in order to maximize profits.

Retail Smart also offers a 3D experience that enables retailers to create three-dimensional store models, including the audio and video components that will be playing in-store. Users are able to understand the entire brand experience, including various sensory elements, to ensure a cohesive branded experience.

Industry trade events

As you know, the retail industry is not static; retailers are continually researching dynamic ways in which to attract and retain customers in a highly competitive marketplace. Trade shows allow retailers and brands to be at the forefront of new opportunities for their brand.

Just as buying teams attend market weeks to learn about seasonal trends and complete seasonal buys, visual merchandising teams attend trade shows to learn about industry trends for merchandising, store planning, and store display. Some of the largest trade shows are GlobalShop (now RetailX), NeoCon, and EuroShop. Merchandisers attend these trade shows to learn about new fixtures and signage, lighting options, décor, props, mannequins. . . you name it, it is there!

What is RetailX?

RetailX is a newly created trade show and conference, bringing together three of the retail industry's top to-the-trade events. RetailX is a partnership between GlobalShop, RFID Journal LIVE! Retail, and Internet Retailer Conference and Exhibition (IRCE). These three shows are held concurrently in one location to give guests the opportunity to attend each show simultaneously.

The focus of RetailX is what retail is today: integrated, responsive, and engaging. RetailX events educate retailers on how to integrate both bricks and clicks into business models in order to tap into new revenue streams and increase market share. Participants gain access to manufacturers for sourcing, industry professionals for networking and collaboration, and educational resources.

Some of the topics attendees learn about include: physical store design, user experience, store planning, marketing, or inventory control and operations to help retailers build a brand and create a more compelling, effective retail experience.

Read below to learn more about the three different trade events that comprise RetailX.

GlobalShop

GlobalShop is the retail industry's largest design and merchandising event for shopper-facing retail design, technology, and in-store marketing. Guests participate in educational sessions led by leaders in the retail industry, learn innovative and emerging trends in store design, planning, construction, and visual merchandising, and have the opportunity to test out new products. GlobalShop is held each year in June at McCormick Place in Chicago.

In order to keep pace with the rapidly changing retail industry, GlobalShop has evolved to include both the digital retail environment as well as brick-and-mortar. This can be seen through GlobalShop's integration into RetailX.

Internet Retailer Conference & Exhibition (IRCE)

The Internet Retailer Conference & Exhibition is the world's largest e-commerce event. The goal is to be a one-stop shop for e-commerce needs. Vendors are on-hand to offer solutions for various business needs, ranging from email marketing to payment to logistics.

The education series provides lectures and workshops addressing existing and emerging issues and trends in the e-commerce space.

RFID Journal LIVE! Retail

RFID Journal LIVE! Retail is a conference that focuses on how radio frequency identification (RFID) is used to improve inventory accuracy, enhance replenishment, and enable omnichannel retailing. Retail industry professionals need to understand how RFID impacts store operations, merchandising strategies, and retailer back-end systems.

Company Spotlight: Visual Retailing

The software MockShop allows planograms and visual directives to be more focused and detailed for each store location, improving brand awareness and product sell-through.

Visual Retailing offers innovative retail solutions to assist brands with a comprehensive retail plan, including store planning, visual merchandising, and retail execution. Utilizing an innovative retail technology within its software programs, Visual Retailing provides retailers and brands the resources they need to thrive in a fast-paced retail environment.

Visual Retailing offers a suite of products and services to best fit their customers' needs:

MockShop creates 3D mockups of stores, including store-specific fixtures and inventory. Retailers are able to create planograms and visual guidelines for stores to follow, ensuring consistency across markets. Once planograms are created, seasonal merchandise can be placed on fixtures to assist with stock management as well as product placement. This ensures that store level teams understand exactly how merchandise should appear on the sales floor throughout the year.

The software MockShop allows planograms and visual directives to be more focused and detailed for each store location, improving brand awareness and product sell-through. Additionally, the 3D mockups work in tandem with heat mapping to better understand sell-through, price balance, or visualize any other data attribute within any specific environment.

ShopShape is a cloud-based solution providing communication between merchandising teams at the corporate offices and store level merchandisers. Data from store locations is stored in the ShopShape dashboard for streamlined communication.

Additionally, store level teams are able to share photos of their sales floor with regional managers/ head office to assist with merchandise and display placement and adherence to corporate directives. Corporate teams are able to assess effectiveness of planograms; all parties are privy to real-time feedback.

4.11   4.12

4.13
StyleShoots includes both hardware and software. StyleShoots machines allow users to take flawless photos and videos to be used for web, social media, or in-store signage. It can be a seamless integration into MockShop and ShopShape, reducing steps and increasing product availability and accessibility.

ShopShape supports MockShop, as it is a platform to share MockShop planograms company-wide. There is no physical travel required and no lag time to see in-store displays in various locations.

ShopShape also offers the capability to create any type of questionnaire/checklist, which can be shared with store teams to connect with and offer merchandising solutions through both text and images and give answers in both text and images back to head office in real time. This digital solution not only saves on printing and transportation costs, but also saves a lot of travel time, with the same insights of your stores in one platform.

SampleRoom is designed for the wholesale process. It is a digital showroom for brands to sell product to their retail customers.

Product is highly visual, allowing retail buyers to see complete collections as well as product data in one place. This ensures a more streamlined seasonal buy as buyers can plan, manage, and execute their buys through one platform.

Products can be viewed three-dimensionally as well as placed on fixtures to allow buyers to envision the product on their sales floor.

Photos can be taken on mannequins, flat lay, or on models, allowing users to get the best photos and videos for their comprehensive range of product offerings. StyleShoots can automatically remove the background from flat-lay and mannequin images to give you free-floating products, to use for any purpose like marketing, e-commerce websites, and many more.

All StyleShoots machines include a built-in top tier Canon camera and an integrated iPad with bespoke software from which users can control everything. These all-in-one tools can take care of the complete content production process for e-commerce studios. Crisp images and cinematic videos are ready for export in a matter of minutes.

Search Visual Retailing to learn more about their products and services.

Who Should Attend RetailX?

Retailers, consumer product companies, retail contract designers, and architects focused on:

- Retail architecture, design and planning
- Consumer insights
- Shopper marketing
- Visual merchandising
- Technology
- Innovation
- Store operations
- Buying/purchasing

What is NeoCon?

NeoCon is tradeshow targeting industry professionals working in commercial design; it focuses on the physical space (i.e., interior design) of a store. The tradeshow is comprised of over 600 exhibitors who are on hand to educate attendees on products and services that will create a functional and aesthetically pleasing commercial environment.

Vendors introducing new trends as well as established products in categories such as furniture, fabrics, flooring, interior building products, interior finishes, and technology are on hand at NeoCon to showcase their goods, discuss product benefits, and provide design solutions.

In addition to exhibitors representing emerging and established products, NeoCon also provides educational opportunities for attendees. Each year NeoCon offers seminars, keynote presentations, and other special programs to educate guests on design trends, business-to-business needs, and business-to-consumer needs.

Since 1969, NeoCon has been held every June at The Merchandise Mart in Chicago.

Who attends?

Attendees at NeoCon span an array of industries, as commercial design is apparent anywhere and everywhere. Participants represent markets ranging from healthcare, hospitality, retail, education, and the public sector.

What is EuroShop?

EuroShop is a retail trade fair held every three years in Dusseldorf, Germany. It is the world's largest trade fair for the retail industry and targets a global audience. The 2017 show featured 2,368 exhibitors from sixty-one countries. There were close to 114,000 visitors from 138 countries visiting eighteen exhibition halls.

The next show will be held in 2020 and will include exhibitors that work across the various facets and channels of the modern retail industry. The 2020 show will focus on eight "Experience Dimensions" which encompass the different facets of the retail industry as we know it: retail marketing, retail technology, expo and event marketing, lighting, food service equipment, visual merchandising, shop fitting and store design, and refrigeration and energy management.

Who attends?

Attendees travel from international locations near and far to participate in EuroShop. They span the various categories of the retail industry.

Summary

Store planning teams are charged with creating engaging, shoppable sales floors that inspire customers to explore all that the brand has to offer. Their role is no longer maximizing inventory on the sales floor. Store planning teams integrate merchandise with in-store experiences and retail technologies while ensuring consistent messaging across platforms.

Brands are using both physical and digital resources to plan, execute, and communicate across departments and retail locations. Many of the virtual resources allow real time communication to streamline processes.

KEY TERMS

EuroShop
Forced path layout
Free-flow
Grid
Herringbone
Loop
NeoCon
RetailX
Selling space
Square footage
Store planning
Transition area

CRITICAL THINKING: THE APPLICATION PROCESS

After completing the chapter readings, reflect on the information and experiences shared. Apply what you learned to future retail experiences:

1. How should retailers prioritize their integration of technologies into the brick-and-mortar shopping experience?
2. What does the integration of digital technologies mean for store planning and store design?
3. How should (or shouldn't) existing and emerging digital technologies be integrated into store design?

5

Store interiors

Overview

Digital technologies have altered the way consumers shop in a variety of ways. The traditional, physical store has to adapt to consumers' changing shopping habits and find new methods of engaging with their customers. With more and more customers shopping online, store interiors reflect new ways in which retailers are working to drive traffic to their store. In-store collaborations between brick-and-mortar stores and e-commerce sites are one way in which the traditional, physical store is adapting to consumers' changing shopping habits. Additionally, the sales floor now includes iPads, oversized screens, kiosks, and charging stations intermixed with live merchandise; retailers rely on these elements to draw customers into the store and off their digital devices. As a result, the sales floor looks quite different than it did just a few years ago.

This chapter will introduce the changing landscape of store interiors, including retail collaborations, the integration of digital technologies on the sales floor, the elimination of cash wraps, experiential retail, and sensory merchandising.

5.1
Alexander McQueen
London, Old Bond
Street. Retailers are now
accounting for in-store
technologies to be
incorporated alongside
merchandise to further
engage shoppers. Screens
and tablets are oftentimes
used to connect shoppers
to fashion shows, branded
social media sites,
e-commerce sites, and
product customization.

Retail collaborations

In order to drive traffic to brick-and-mortar stores, retailers are collaborating with pure play e-tailers in hopes to attract a new market to the in-store shopping experience. This greatly impacts in-store merchandising strategies, as the sales floor is no longer dedicated solely to selling the retailer's inventory.

In 2017, Kohl's launched The Amazon Experience at ten of Kohl's stores throughout the United States. The Amazon Experience was a partnership between the Wisconsin-based retailer and Amazon to offer various Amazon products and services within Kohl's brick-and-mortar stores. With the average Kohl's shopper between the ages of 35 and 44, the retailer was looking for ways to attract Millennial customers to their stores. The retailer's partnership with Amazon is the first step in attracting a new generation of shoppers to Kohl's stores. The strategic partnership between Kohl's and Amazon began when Kohl's accepted returns from Amazon purchases in select Kohl's stores even though products were not purchased at Kohl's.

The partnership evolved as Kohl's is now acting as a physical selling outlet for Amazon branded products. Kohl's originally housed Amazon kiosks in a limited number of stores, but recently shuttered these kiosks in favor of a more customer-centric approach. Amazon branded products (i.e., Alexa) now have permanent, dedicated floor space and are sold directly to customers through Kohl's brick-and-mortar stores. The Amazon products are merchandised in their own location on the selling floor, drawing a lot of attention due to the clean lines and limited inventory on the sales floor (which is very different from the rest of the store).

Why are retailers putting these external partnerships front and forward? Yes, it is all about getting shoppers into the store. Inviting Amazon customers into Kohl's stores for convenient returns drives a younger customer base to the store. Remember what we said the biggest challenge retailers face? (Hint: getting customers into the store!) Well, Kohl's is now getting an entirely new batch of customers to venture into their stores. These customers visit Kohl's with the intention of simply returning their Amazon purchases, but, after meandering through the store to the customer service desk to complete their return, they have passed by thousands of products along the way. If they don't make a purchase that day, they have at least become aware of the depth and breadth of Kohl's product offerings.

Experiential retail

Today's consumers are choosing to spend their hard-earned money on experiences rather than products; as a result, retailers are amending their business models to include opportunities for their customers to participate in branded experiences within the brick-and-mortar stores.

What is the benefit of experiential retail? It gives customers the opportunity to test out products before making a purchase. Customers are better able to understand the benefits received from products as they have used them in the context in which they are meant to be used. For example, Williams Sonoma, an American retailer that sells kitchenwares and home furnishings, offers in-store cooking classes. Each class has a different theme, allowing customers to continually test different products, ranging from utensils and appliances

5.2
At the Under Armour Brand House in Chicago, shoppers are invited to test their athleticism and jumping abilities through UA Record. They can then download the UA Record app to continue their relationship with Under Armour by setting goals, logging activities, and connecting with friends and athletes, all while sharing this data with Under Armour for product recommendations and promotions.

to sauces, spices, and mixes. Participants not only acquire in-depth information about the products, but they also become more comfortable with an array of products sold by the retailer. An added bonus? Most classes provide participants a one-time discount on purchases made after the class, incentivizing participants to take advantage of discounted prices and make a purchase.

The Williams Sonoma workshops require participants to plan ahead by registering for the class, but other retailers incorporate in-store experiences in a more organic way. Apple has created store environments that entice customers to stop in and truly experience the wide range of products and services that are for sale. Rather than pushing product recommendations out to customers, Apple is pulling customers in; think about this as an "opt in" versus "opt out." By pulling customers into the store, shoppers are choosing to engage with the brand rather than advertisements or sales tactics that push (sometimes unwanted) information out to customers. Upon entering an Apple store, customers notice perfectly symmetrical rows of tables displaying Apple products. Tables are not cluttered by additional inventory, boxes, or complementary products; products are easily accessible. There are no barriers in place to test the products as they are plugged in (meaning, always fully charged), turned on, and void of password requirements; they are loaded with an array of apps, photos, and videos to demonstrate product capabilities. Visitors to Apple stores are invited to add their own content (with varying levels of permissions) to products as well. As customers wander throughout the store, it is nearly impossible to not engage with the highly accessible Apple products. These touchpoints create an emotional connection between the customers and merchandise as shoppers are able to connect the products to their lifestyle.

Additionally, Apple stores offer an array of educational classes, product support, and special events for customers to maximize their usage and efficiency with Apple products as well as engage with the brand. In 2019, Apple launched "Today at Apple" educational sessions at Apple stores worldwide. These events invite Apple experts and members of the community to participate, creating a sense of community in the retail space. Although educational courses require participants to register ahead of time, oftentimes in-store customers share in the experience as videos and images are projected in the store or musical productions are heard overhead. For example, in 2019, an educational course entitled "Music Lab: Building Your Song Co-created with Florence Welch" was held at the Michigan Avenue (Chicago, Illinois) store. As the class ran, an oversized screen projected the work in progress to a stadium-style seating area filled with Apple customers. Discussions from the class and the music that was being created echoed in the background. Whether they were interested in the coursework or simply taking time to sit for a few minutes, the seats were filled; Apple had created a welcoming, inviting atmosphere for shoppers.

However, not all in-store experiences are in the form of organized classes. Many examples of experiential retail invite customers to explore the brands and test the products at their leisure throughout the shopping experience. One of the most talked about retail experiences from 2018 was Canada Goose's Cold Room. Canada Goose, a luxury outerwear brand, created an in-store experience that emphasized product functionality. Built into existing Canada Goose stores, the Cold Room is a small room surrounded by ice sculptures; the temperature is set to –27

5.3
The retail environment at Apple stores invites customers to explore and experience their products, allowing customers to connect with brand and product offerings.

5.4
A workshop at the Apple store teaches guests how to create their own song using various Apple products. Although participants register for the workshops, workshops are held in community spaces, enabling Apple customers to listen and observe.

degrees Fahrenheit. On any given day, lines wrapped around the store as customers tested the limits of their chosen Canada Goose cold weather products inside the Cold Room. A novel experience, many participants were not Canada Goose customers, but rather simply wanted to experience the Cold Room. This is still a win for the brand as Canada Goose has not only gotten shoppers into their store, but they have also gotten them into their merchandise. They might not be in the market for a $1,000+ coat right now, but perhaps they are future Canada Goose customers. When they are in the market for a winter coat, the Cold Room experience will be at the top of their minds.

Casper, a mattress retailer, offers "The Dreamery" in their New York City showroom to allow customers the opportunity to test out Casper mattresses. The Dreamery includes "nap pods" where customers schedule a forty-five minute nap to test out mattresses sold at the store. Casper provides pajamas and soothing music for participants to help users relax and unwind before taking their scheduled nap. With a large purchase like a mattress, customers are able to really experience the product in the very way in which it will be used. (And what's not to love about a mid-day scheduled nap?!)

British retailer John Lewis has reduced selling space in order to integrate "experience

5.5
At John Lewis' new concept store in Southampton (United Kingdom), customers are invited to interact with products in order to not only learn more about merchandise offerings but also learn from industry experts.

playgrounds" into the brick-and-mortar shopping experience. The experience playgrounds are found on each floor of the multi-floor department store and focus on different categories of the retailer's product offerings. Some experiences require participant registration (i.e., pasta making class) while others invite shoppers to explore at their leisure (i.e., stay and play gadget area). This new concept store opened at the end of 2019, but John Lewis is not new to integrating in-store experiences with brick-and-mortar shopping.

In 2017, John Lewis launched a campaign entitled "National Treasures" to highlight "the best of British life, design and culture." The purpose of the National Treasures campaign was to attract customers to the stores to see, learn, experience, make, and dine; the retail store was turned into a place of discovery for participants. The campaign relied on nostalgia as shoppers could relate to most, if not all, the scenarios depicted throughout the campaign. The goal was for John Lewis to connect with their British customer base by celebrating some of the UK's favorite things, pastimes, and quirks about what it means to spend the summer in the United Kingdom. Store windows promoted the entire National Treasures campaign, ranging from whimsical illustrations to event promotions. The windows featured colorful illustrations by British illustrator Paul Thurlby, depicting traditions like ice cream by the seaside and afternoons in the park, and also promoted a series of events in which John Lewis partnered with over 100 local businesses to host events and workshops throughout the summer. The windows did not feature any sellable merchandise, as the goal was to entice shoppers to participate in the National Treasures campaign, creating an emotional connection with customers, leading customers to stop inside the John Lewis "destination for discovery" store.

In-store displays supported the campaign by incorporating life-sized cutouts of the characters featured in the illustrations as well as additional illustrations throughout the store for cohesive messaging. Customers also shopped a "national treasury" pop-up shop that featured iconic British brands such as Mulberry, Hunter, and Dyson as well as limited edition products featuring Thurlby's illustrations.

Customers were able to further explore the campaign by participating in any of the 1,000 events offered throughout the United Kingdom. For example, the brand's flagship Oxford Street (London) location hosted fitness and gardening classes on the rooftop. These in-store events allowed John Lewis stores to draw people into the physical stores for an experience, improving the relationship between the retailer and the customer, while also exposing participants to products sold in-store.

These are just a few examples demonstrating how the shopping experience has become less transactional and more experiential. Shoppers are spending more time in stores, increasing their exposure and awareness of not only product offerings but also product benefits. There is no longer a sales pitch involved to convince shoppers to make a purchase; shoppers have had the opportunity to use products and are well versed in the benefits received.

Visual merchandisers are creating retail environments that emphasize the in-store experience rather than the sellable product. This reduces inventory levels on the sales floor and increases the points of connection between the retailer and shopper.

Company Spotlight: Reformation

Not only is Reformation an eco-friendly women's retailer, but they are also well known for creating a brick-and-mortar store that replicates the online shopping experience. Touchscreens are highly visible and accessible throughout the store, integrated in the architecture and infrastructure in order to provide a radically personalized shopping experience for customers.

While the focus of their merchandise is sustainability, the in-store experience is tech-based. The goal of Reformation's brick-and-mortar experience is to create an in-store shopping experience that closely aligns with shopping online.

The in-store experience relies heavily on digital technologies, as there are iPads and oversized digital screens throughout the store, intertwined with racks of clothing. Throughout the store, racks of product are neatly merchandised to display one of each item, making it much easier for customers to shop the products. Each item feels special and luxurious, as it is not crammed alongside an array of other product. When a customer is interested in trying on or purchasing a garment, a sales associate, armed with an iPhone, is able to quickly scan the barcode on the hangtag for product availability. If the garment is available in the requested size and/or color, it will be virtually added to their fitting room or simply rung up.

How does it work?

The sales associate scans the desired item, choosing which size(s); it notifies the stock room which garment needs to be pulled. Without being weighted down by personal items and in-store products, customers can take their time perusing the store before heading to try items on.

Once the customer has completed their shopping, their fitting room wardrobe is stocked with their requested merchandise.

Another option for customers is to shop via the in-store tablets and screens. Just like the online shopping experience, customers scroll through Reformation's website and select the desired garments. Inventory is updated in real time so customers truly are shopping available inventory. Desired items are added to the shopper's virtual fitting room. When their shopping is complete, customers have the option of either trying the garments on or making an immediate purchase.

If they would like to try garments on, they choose the option to create a fitting room; garments will be added to their fitting room and they will be notified when their room is ready. Customers are able to continually add to their fitting room independently, or with the help of a sales associate, by simply choosing "add to existing fitting room."

When customers are ready to try on their items, they are brought to the fitting room, where the garments are housed inside a "magic wardrobe," or a minimalistic dresser that feels like you are at home. The magic wardrobe also features a small digital screen for continued communication with the Reformation team members. The closets are an important part of the Reformation shopping experience as they allow product to be unobtrusively added to the fitting room upon the request of the customer.

Remember the last time you tried on something in a fitting room, loved it, but the size was way off? Either you were swimming in it or felt squeezed in it? Neither is a good look; you likely did not want to venture out onto the sales floor to swap out the size. Instead, you were held captive in the fitting room until a sales associate made their way back. Unfortunately, there are few options if a sales associate is not accessible to grab you the requested size. Reformation has (geniusly) solved this problem. When customers want a different item, they use the tablet inside the fitting room to choose the new item(s) they wish to try on. The audio on the tablet tells the shopper to close the doors of the in-room magic wardrobe; once the doors are closed, a Reformation employee opens a door from the back to place new items inside.

Products are added to the closets via a magnetic door that opens one side at a time. This ensures privacy between the fitting room and stock room. The typical wait time for a new garment? Ninety seconds! And just like that, a new size or complementary product has been delivered to the room.

In-room tablets are not the only way the fitting rooms are digitally connected. The smart fitting rooms allow shoppers to adjust lighting based on time of day and/or occasion garment will be worn. Lighting options include Cool, Golden, and Sexy-time. Customers are invited to plug in their mobile devices to listen to music of their choice as they try garments on, creating a more personalized experience. Phones can also be charged while shoppers are in the fitting room.

When customers wrap up their shopping, the checkout process is, not surprising, mobile and wireless; there is not a single cash wrap in sight. To reduce the typical cash wrap clutter, Reformation does not accept cash, allowing customers to swipe their credit card using a small, discreet card reader.

5.6
Inside Reformation's Chicago store, touchscreens are seamlessly integrated throughout the sales floor to create a brick-and-mortar shopping experience that closely resembles the online shopping experience.

Sensory merchandising

As the retail environment evolves to include active experiences for shoppers, you will notice that this is a process that incorporates our five senses. How does the brick-and-mortar shopping experience integrate our five senses?

Think about your last experience shopping in a brick-and-mortar store. What brought you there? Was it destination shopping . . . you knew exactly what you wanted and/or needed and you were in and out of the store in the blink of an eye? Did you buy online, but visit the store for in-store pickup? Did the window display catch your eye and steer you into the store? What sounds did you hear when you entered the store? The ringing of the cash register, the clanking of rolling racks, or hangers knocking against fixtures? Or was there background music, a DJ spinning, or in-store performer? And the smell. . . candles? Perfume? Coffee? Baked goods? And what about your in-store experience? Was there an area where you could sit down and relax for a few minutes in a comfy seating area? Run on a treadmill or climb a rock-climbing wall? Did you grab a coffee or a snack? Watch a fashion show, TV show, or video giving you product knowledge for the brand or retailer? Did the retailer use a POS system on a mobile device? Although this is a seemingly long list, it is certainly not an exhaustive list of how one's senses are activated while shopping. These are just a few examples of how our senses are engaged while shopping in brick-and-mortar retailers.

As you see, retail design has become a **multi-sensory experience**. According to "The Multichannel Merchant," by engaging all five senses in the merchandising experience, retailers create a memory that connects positively into their customer's emotional bank.

Let's take a few minutes to review how retailers utilize sensory engagement in the shopping experience.

Sight: First and foremost, retail is a visual experience. If we see something appealing and attractive, we are eager to explore. This is not simply the product itself; we make our first impressions of a store based on what we see as soon as we approach a store. Consider the store exterior, ranging from façade to lighting to signage. If the façade, window, signage, or other exterior elements are not visually appealing, we assume that interior elements, including store merchandise, will feel much the same. For example, a ripped awning, burnt out lights and dirty windows give the

5.7
An in-store display for Dyson products engages shoppers' senses through sight, sound, and touch. Retailers are changing store formats, offering in-store experiences to attract customers as e-commerce has disrupted the industry.

impression that store itself has not been well cared for, including store merchandise. Sight is our most dominant sense: this affects not only our desire to enter the store, but ultimately, our willingness to make a purchase and the price point we are willing to pay.

Sound: What sounds did you hear when you entered the store? Sales associates being paged? Soothing music? Chattering customers? Sound is an important part of the ambiance of the retail environment. Background music sets a tone for customer perception of their overall shopping experience and expectation. If done correctly, music reflects the brand's personality, enhances the customer experience, and increases sales.

If a store is playing music, 84 percent of US consumers cite that "the shopping experience is more enjoyable," 81 percent say that their "mood is lifted," and 70 percent express that they "feel like it's a brand they can relate and connect to" (In-Store, Atmosphere Counts, 2017).

5.8
The Lucky Brand store feels welcoming and inviting as the store name is fully illuminated, doors are propped open, and exterior windows display seasonally appropriate product.

Music selections must be thoughtful as tempo, volume, and genre impact shopping behavior.

The music played at your favorite retailer affects not only the amount of time customers spend in a store, but also the pace at which they navigate through the store and their overall mood while shopping. There is a direct correlation between the amount of time spent in a store and purchases made: the longer we spend in a store, the more money we spend.

Music that is a faster tempo speeds up the rate at which people navigate through a store. The faster we move, the less product we are looking at, reducing the opportunity to make impulse purchases. On the other hand, slower-paced music reduces the speed at which consumers navigate a store, giving them more time to really look around at displays, fixtures, and merchandising strategies. The opportunity for upselling and impulse purchases is greatly increased.

Another important consideration for retail store playlists is the brand's target customer. Music selections should be tailored to the target market. Research shows that when people hear music they like, they are more likely to make a purchase.

Customers' perception of timing and time spent in store is also affected by the genre of music heard overhead. Customers who listen to music they like are more apt to feel as if they had a positive shopping experience, even if they had to wait in line to check out or talk to a customer service associate. A simple and inexpensive solution to keeping customers happy: play the right music and they won't mind waiting!

The genre of music played also influences consumers in regards to perception of the store, merchandise and price expectations. For example, at a wine store, customers chose more expensive bottles when classical musical was played within the store. Shoppers associated classical music with sophistication and high-quality products, which directly translated to the merchandise offering and pricing strategies.

Everlane, a direct-to-consumer fashion label that recently opened brick-and-mortar stores throughout the United States, uses sound in a completely different way to engage shoppers. The brand is best known for selling ethically made goods and offering radical transparency regarding how their products are made; they wanted to translate the concept they are most known for (transparency) to their brick-and-mortar stores. The Everlane website is full of information about how their products are made, the factories they work with, and a complete cost breakdown for each garment. In order to ensure this same information is available throughout their brick-and-mortar stores, Everlane provides headphones with "transparency moments" for customers to learn about how and where products are made.

Sephora is using sound to cultivate connections with customers who subscribe to their Play! By Sephora monthly beauty boxes. Each monthly beauty box will include a Spotify playlist with a curated list of songs that coincide with the monthly theme of the box. This reinforces the relationship between sound and shopping experience.

Touch: Shoppers are using brick-and-mortar stores to not only make purchases but also as a way to research products before making online purchases. Seventy-eight percent of global customers shop brick-and-mortar stores so they can touch, feel, and try on products. More than 55 percent of consumers visit stores before buying online, reinforcing the idea that tactile experience plays an important role in the consumer decision-making process. Although e-commerce, s-commerce, and m-commerce allow consumers to shop anywhere at any time, there is still a big draw for consumers to visit brick-and-mortar retailers. Sixty-six percent of female and 59 percent of male shoppers are drawn to brick-and-mortar stores because they can decipher color, fit, and texture of products in a more discerning way than digital shopping platforms allow (Skrovan, 2017).

Smell: Scent motivates the average shopper to linger longer and subconsciously connect with brands more quickly. According to a study by Nike, a scent in-store can increase a shopper's intent to purchase by 80 percent. Similarly, a brand-appropriate smell can encourage shoppers to spend up to 20 percent more time in-store and almost 75 percent of people have been drawn into a store by an inviting smell. The challenge for stores then becomes how they can leverage the impact of scent to help create a service-orientated, experiential, and personalized in-store experience. Anthropologie, part of the URBN Inc. brand, has a cult-like following for the signature smell in their brick-and-mortar locations. Although they sell a variety of candles to consumers, they use one specific candle as their signature scent in every store location. Enter any Anthropologie location and you will find their signature Capri Blue Volcano candle burning in close proximity to the store entrance(s) to draw in passersby; the same candle is burning throughout the store and fitting rooms to make customers feel at ease. In fact, employees light in-store candles thirty minutes before store opening to ensure the scent has matriculated throughout the entire store.

Much like the relationship between music and buying behavior, there is also a direct correlation between scent and buying behavior. A recent study found that in clothing stores, the sale of women's clothing doubled when feminine scents such as vanilla were used. Similarly, the sales of men's clothing rose significantly when male scents such as rose maroc or patchouli were introduced (Khan, 2016).

What does this mean for retail environments? Know your customer! If your store is gender specific, seek out a gender-targeted fragrance to see a significant increase in over-all sales.

Jewelry store Pandora introduced ambient scenting in its stores to enhance the customer shopping experience with the goal of creating an unforgettable atmosphere. The results? The perception of the brand was enhanced and customers shared their positive opinions of the scent, demonstrating the power of choosing the right scent for your brand.

How can various scented products be incorporated throughout the store? Merchandising teams must consider if the scented product is part of store inventory or simply a branding opportunity, as you don't want to confuse customers. If the scented product is part of the store inventory, oftentimes it is considered an add-on purchase. As a result, it should be found throughout the store, merchandised alongside complementary products. For example, loungewear and candles merchandised as product adjacencies promote a sense of relaxation. Additionally, scented products should be housed on high-capacity fixtures near cash wraps to subtly remind customers to make a quick and easy add-on purchase.

If scented products are not part of the store inventory, as seen in the Pandora example, then be sure it is clear to customers that these products are not for sale. This could mean candles and infusers are found only at the cash wrap or in fitting rooms or room sprays are inconspicuously used throughout the day. The only scented product a customer will find is product in use (i.e., a singular burning candle) but any additional candles are behind closed doors (stock rooms, cash wrap drawers, and cabinets) so it does not appear to be back stock.

Taste: Although not every store sells merchandise that can be taste-tested, it doesn't mean that, at the very least, food and/or beverage can't be integrated in the shopping experience! Think about the last time you were shopping; during the shopping excursion, it is likely that you (or one of your shopping companions) became hungry or thirsty. You planned on making a quick trip to grab a snack and then return to continue your shopping. . . only you decided to move on and continue shopping elsewhere. Sound familiar? Customers often leave stores with the intention of returning to continue their shopping but decide against it once they have exited the store. (Remember that we mentioned early on in the text that a retailer's biggest challenge is actually getting shoppers to walk through their doors? Now,

5.9
A birds-eye view of the dining room at RH Chicago, The Gallery at The Three Arts Club, where guests are immersed in RH product throughout their dining experience.

imagine having to do that twice for the same customer!). This is why retailers are incorporating restaurants, bars, and coffee shops into their shopping environments. . . the longer a customer stays in a store, the more money they are likely to spend!

In 2015, Restoration Hardware completely changed their business model as they shifted from a traditional retail environment to an experiential showroom model. Rebranded RH, the American housewares company created design galleries that "are more home than store and inspire a new way of living" (rh.com). Their flagship locations not only feature comprehensive product offerings from their various collections (RH Interiors, RH Modern, RH Teen, RH Baby and Child, and their outdoor collections), but they also include restaurants where customers are surrounded by RH products during their dining experience. Everything in the restaurant,

from the tables and chairs to chandeliers and outdoor decor, is part of the brand's product assortment. Additionally, some locations also include bakeries and coffee shops that welcome visitors to stop in for a coffee to-go or have a seat in a more casual environment than the dining room, all while surrounded by RH products that are available for sale. The goal is that customers use the products, fall in love, then immediately place an order for their furniture products to be delivered to their home. Because these design galleries do not stock inventory for customers to walk out of the store with their purchases, the stores do not need to dedicate square footage to stock rooms, allowing for more selling space and opportunity for in-store experiences.

At the Chicago RH store, 15 percent of the first floor's square footage is dedicated to an in-store dining experience. This includes a sit-down restaurant (3 Arts Club Café), coffee bar and bakery, and wine bar. Customers are comfortably seated at RH dining room tables and chairs, enjoy a cup of coffee or tea, and sample wine, before or after they have strolled throughout the multi-level design center, merchandised by room and theme.

Crate and Barrel is taking this one step further in their in-store restaurants, with the goal of creating a truly immersive shopping experience for customers. The Plate at Crate and Barrel, launched in 2019, allows guests to enjoy a dining experience that fully integrates products currently on the sales floor and available for purchase. Not only will customers be comfortably seated at Crate and Barrel dining room tables and chairs, but the coffee brewed will be made using small kitchen appliances sold at Crate and Barrel and customers will sip their beverages from Crate and Barrel mugs. Tabletop décor, including plates, glasses, and cutlery will not only create an ambiance in the restaurant, but will also be found just steps away on the sales floor. Crate and Barrel hopes the dining experience will inspire guests and show them how the products sold throughout the store fit into their everyday lifestyle at home.

Other retailers like Ikea, Club Monaco, Uniqlo, and Target are including coffee shops, bakeries and restaurants in smaller scales within their stores in order to keep customers shopping in-store as long as possible. If retailers don't have the square footage to offer a full restaurant, then they may simply choose to offer shoppers a bottled water, coffee, or tea while customers are shopping. For example, back in Chapter 2, we introduced smart mirrors. At the Rebecca Minkoff flagship store in New York City, customers use a smart mirror to place an order from a limited menu of beverage options to be enjoyed as they peruse the store. Once the order is received, the beverage is delivered directly to the shopper while they are browsing (or, even better, in the fitting room trying on!).

Retailers are also partnering with local businesses for cross-promotional opportunities. For example, when New York's Magnolia Bakery opened their doors in Chicago, they partnered with BHLDN, the bridal division of URBN Inc., to create awareness of their new bakery location. BHLDN used cake stands and plates from their housewares department to strategically display baked goods from Magnolia Bakery throughout the store, inviting BHLDN customers to sample sweets from the newly opened bakery. Not only did this increase exposure for Magnolia Bakery, but it also allowed shoppers to snack while they shopped, keeping them in the store longer and creating an emotional connection with both brands. The baked goods from Magnolia Bakery also acted as a suggestive selling tool, reminding shoppers at the bridal store that they will need a dessert at their wedding, and why not hire the bakery for their wedding needs!

By integrating all five senses into the shopping environment, the brick-and-mortar retail environment has evolved to experiential retail. If shoppers are going to open their wallets, they want an experience alongside their purchase. Shoppers are no longer visiting a store for a transactional purchase; the brick-and-mortar experience is a way for brands and shoppers to build a relationship.

Shoppers want to engage with the brand in order to connect with not only the merchandise, but also the marketing, design, and buying processes. This can be done through interactive experiences in the store, both through physical and digital interactions.

Sensing technology

Retailers integrate sensing technology in stores to promote products and share product knowledge with shoppers. **Sensing technology** utilizes sensors to understand activity that is going on around them. Sensors detect and respond to activity from the physical environment; typically this "activity" is movement.

Perch Interactive is one such example that unites physical products with digital content to engage shoppers through sensing technology. Perch Interactive offers a technology that incorporates physical activity with an active brand experience, not just from a consumer perspective to drive sales, but also allowing retailers and brands to analyze consumer behavior.

Perch Interactive creates displays that merge physical products with digital interactions; their programs enable shoppers to merge the tactile shopping experience with the digital media they have become accustomed to in their daily lives. These digital interactions use sensing technology to detect when shoppers touch physical product; it is at this moment the Perch Interactive technology provides product information to engage the customer. Timeliness is of the utmost importance because the tactile experience is the critical moment when a shopper becomes a potential customer as they consider making a purchase.

Macy's and Perch Interactive partnered to create a more interactive experience for in-store fragrance purchases. The 3D sensing technology senses when a bottle has been touched, digitally providing product highlights to shoppers to allow them to better understand not just the product itself, but the story behind it. Using **computer vision**, as customers touch fragrance bottles or testers, digital content, such as branded videos, ratings, and reviews, and fragrance notes, are automatically activated. Computer vision, closely linked with artificial intelligence, is when computers identify and interpret information from images and 3D and then take action in some way.

This in-store experience, integrating the physical store and product along with digital experiences, is a strong differentiator between shopping online and shopping brick-and-mortar. Now, in the physical store environment, customers can hold the bottle, test the scents, and learn about the fragrance through digital interactions. They not only become more informed and educated every time they pick up a fragrance bottle, but they are engaged in an active shopping experience. With the tap of a screen, information is streamed to customers. Taking it one step further, when shoppers have found their perfect scent, they can, once again, simply

tap the screen for a QR code to initiate the checkout process.

This experience is mutually beneficial for Macy's as well as their shoppers. As Macy's gains valuable insights into shopper behavior, such as product interest, conversion rates, and dwell time, shoppers have connected with a variety of brands and fragrances and are able to make informed decisions.

Touchscreens: mass customization

Touchscreens allow shoppers to customize products based on their likes and dislikes, wants and needs. The use of touch screens for product customization reduces inventory levels found on sales floor as well as eliminates the need for sales associates to walk customers through the range of product offerings.

Customization allows shoppers to create one-of-a-kind products based on their choices for color, texture, pattern, and overall finish; there are no limitations to what can be done. It speaks to the lifestyle, likes, and dislikes of the customer. Additionally, as the customer creates the product, they are also building a relationship with the brand. Product customization creates an active shopping experience where customers create a product that no one else will have.

Mass customization, on the other hand, allows retailers to offer a menu of options for users to customize products or services. There are limitations to the design process in that there might be one or two styles, five or six colors, and a handful of embellishments; this makes the manufacturing process more manageable, yet users still feel like they have designed their own one-of-a-kind product. For example, jewelry designer Kendra Scott invites shoppers to customize products through The Color Bar. This process relies on in-store touchscreens to execute product customization. It is a three-step process for shoppers to design products ranging from jewelry, to home décor, bridal, and charms. The first step invites shoppers to explore The Color Bar to see the different products that can be customized. After choosing the category in which they want to customize,

5.10 and 5.11
The use of tablets at the customization station at the American Girl store allows shoppers to work independently to create a custom doll and accessories. Customers spend as much or as little time as needed to finalize their decisions.

shoppers choose from over fifty brand styles to customize their chosen product. The third and final step is the customization process, where shoppers choose from over thirty gemstones and the finishing metal. Once the design and customization process is complete, an in-store associate will create the piece, allowing the

shopper to leave with their customized product a few minutes later. As you see, products have been customized based on the customer's requests, but Kendra Scott has established limitations to what the customer is able to do.

This customization process allows users to connect with the Kendra Scott brand by allowing them to create products "just for them"; the idea is that it is unlikely that anyone else will have that exact item. The benefit to Kendra Scott is multi-faceted. They do not have to stock every product combination possible, although every product combination is available to customers. Additionally, Kendra Scott is also gaining market research about what combinations shoppers are creating.

The American Girl store is another retailer that offers shoppers the opportunity to use in-store tablets to customize merchandise. The American Girl store allows shoppers to customize dolls as well as fashion apparel for their dolls. They have dedicated substantial square footage within the store for shoppers to explore product customization, as there are several customization stations available. The in-store set-up encourages shoppers to stop by and have fun discovering the various ways they can customize American Girl dolls, regardless of their intent to purchase. Signage is clear and inviting as it directs customers to "Create a doll that matches your style and spirit" and "Design one of a kind apparel," in case one of the seventy or more existing dolls is not a good fit for the shopper. The signage and digital processes are clear and straightforward, eliminating the need to work with a sales associate to complete the process. The customization process allows shoppers to choose hair color and style, skin tone, face shape, eye color, facial details (freckles, braces, hearing aids, glasses), outfits, accessories, and lastly, customize the doll's personality by adding identifying details such as name, favorite place, favorite things, and pets. Given the customization options for these dolls, there are over thirteen million possible combinations, making it highly likely that your customized doll is truly one of a kind. However, there are limitations in terms of customization options. Customers pay a premium for the customized dolls as they start at $200 USD, whereas other American Girl dolls are $115 USD for the doll and corresponding book.

What do these customization stations mean for visual merchandisers? Customized products are often sold at a higher price point because of the individualized nature of the goods. Therefore, customization stations should feel like a specialty area within the store. They should be easily accessible, ensuring shoppers can seamlessly transition from browsing tangible products to virtually customizing their own products. Oftentimes shoppers who customize products are not looking for sales assistance; instead, they prefer to work independently to create a one-of-a-kind product that meets their needs. This means the customization station is used both to educate as well as design. Signage must be clear, concise, and effective, ensuring the users' questions have been answered proactively.

Touchscreens: community engagement

In addition to providing customization options, touchscreens are also used to share information about the brand with users. Nike created a Social Community Wall to not only highlight Nike products, but to also build a community within their customer base. The in-store screen was designed to offer customers the opportunity to immerse themselves in Nike product *and* be inspired by Nike users. The screen features community meet-ups, personal appearances by athletes, inspirational videos, merchandise, and current events; information can be specific to the different geographic locations of Nike stores.

The Social Community Wall is prominently displayed in-store to capture brick-and-mortar customers and refer them back to Nike's digital points of connection. From a merchandising perspective, the digital wall makes a statement; it is a high impact addition to the store that stands alone. There needs to be enough space for shoppers to use the screen but also not act as a bottleneck within the store. Fixtures also need to be placed in such a way that they do not encroach on the screen, both in functionality and visibility. Content is visible from virtually any location in the store.

As you see, these interactive displays are possible, but they are used much less frequently than mobile in-store tech experiences. . . it is certainly not the norm. Retailers have the ability to engage with customers in order to attract unintentional shoppers, creating both brand and product awareness; it reinvigorates the shopping experience. However, it cannot be done alone; it requires cross-disciplinary collaboration, whether retailers are incorporating in-store tech or sensory experiences. Marketing, merchandising, and IT teams must closely work together to ensure user-friendly experience.

Adjustable (customizable) lighting

As shoppers are looking for day-to-night looks, retailers are using digital technologies to adjust lighting in mirrors and fitting rooms to demonstrate how garments look at different times of the day. Shoppers are able to control and adjust lighting based on their needs and/or to reflect when garments will be worn. For example, at Reformation stores, shoppers can adjust fitting room lighting from golden to cool or sexy time to see how garments look in different lighting. Adjusting the light switch allows shoppers to get a better idea of how the garments appear at the different times of the day based on when the garments will be worn.

PerfectScene is one such company that helps retailers create fitting rooms that offer added benefits to shoppers, one benefit being customizable fitting room lighting. Inside the fitting room, customers have a control panel that allows them to alter the fitting room lights to simulate the time of day and/or occasion in which they will be wearing the garments (daylight, home, or night out). The temperature (cool, warm, white) of the lighting adjusts to the shoppers' selections, providing a more accurate impression of the garments, resulting in more informed purchase decisions and fewer returns.

When customers are able to adjust the lights throughout their shopping experience, visual merchandising teams must be aware of other environmental factors, such as wall color and decorative elements. The key here is to simplify. Lighting can be cool (bluish tones) or warm (yellow casts), so a soft white wall ensures that the appearance of products is not affected by the backdrop. The simplicity of the background also ensures that the look of the products is not influenced by bold furniture and décor.

Mobile cash wraps

The last step in the purchasing process, and really the last impression a customer has of a retailer, is the checkout process. It used to be a customer expectation that this final step in the purchasing process concluded at a cash wrap. Customers would gather their items and make their way to a bulky, oversized desk where they would patiently (or not-so-patiently) wait in line to be rung up. Oftentimes while waiting in line, customers would be exposed to **point-of-purchase items** or last minute add-ons to their purchase. Retailers realized they had a captive audience during this time, so it was ideal for messaging and impulse buys. Retailers worked to keep customers distracted while waiting to be rung up so shoppers didn't realize they were actually waiting. However, customer expectations have changed, and we have become accustomed to instant gratification. This translates to consumer behavior in that shoppers don't want to wait. . . not to look for an item and certainly not to complete a purchase. As a result, retailers and tech companies are working to streamline this process to make it more convenient for customers. More and more retailers are findings ways to eliminate the freestanding cash wrap and bring the checkout process directly to the customer. Why is this so important? As we discussed in Chapter 1, oftentimes cash wraps are bulky; they take up valuable real estate on the sales floor. Eliminating the cash wrap allows retailers to gain square footage to be used

for in-store experiences, tech integration, or seating areas, among other things.

However, even more important than gaining square footage is the opportunity to improve the customer experience. As you learned earlier, shoppers' number one complaint is having to wait in line. Eliminating the need to wait in line to complete a purchase simplifies the checkout process, increasing efficiency for both the customer and sales associate.

Customers can now be rung up from anywhere in the store, be it through the retailer's **mobile checkout system** or a third-party system. Retailers like Target, Wal-Mart, Macy's, and Nordstrom utilize their own branded mobile checkout systems, allowing customers to shop, scan, and complete their purchase from anywhere in the store. Other retailers partner with third-party systems in order to provide a mobile checkout system for their customers. Companies like Futureproof Retail and Moltin have created mobile checkout software programs that retailers and consumers can download and use in-store to simplify the checkout process.

Retailers using mobile checkout systems arm their sales associates with mobile devices that act as point of sale systems. Once customers have completed their shopping, sales associates simply scan merchandise through mobile devices to activate the checkout process, no matter where in the store shoppers find themselves. Receipts can be printed via Bluetooth printers or sent electronically via email or text messaging.

Other retailers are empowering customers to shop independently by utilizing software programs that eliminate the need for store associates to close out the sale.

Futureproof Retail is an app that customers download and are able to use at participating retailers. When shopping at participating retailers, customers activate the app when they are ready to make a purchase; they simply scan the item and bag it while shopping. When their shopping is complete, all that is left to do is walk out the door. Payment has been made through a credit card or mobile wallet directly through the app. Simple and straightforward for the customer, but from a loss prevention perspective, there are challenges.

Store associates are responsible for knowing which customers are using the mobile checkout system and which customers will need to be rung up. In a store with less square footage, this is not as challenging, but as the sales floor increases, so does the responsibility of the sales team.

Moltin is another company that has created a third-party app to be used as a mobile point of sale system. Moltin has created a software program that enables shoppers to turn their own smartphone into a point of sale system without needing to take the time to download an app. Using Apple Pay, Google Pay, or a credit card, shoppers are able to shop, scan, and pay right from their mobile devices. Stance, a retailer focused on selling socks, has been using the self-service checkout from Moltin in their brick-and-mortar stores.

What does the process look like? In order to begin the checkout process using Moltin, customers must type in the unique URL that corresponds to the geographic location of the Stance store. For example, customers in the Los Angeles store use la.stance.com. From there, the screen on their mobile device turns into a camera and they scan their items to be rung up. Customers follow the simple prompts on their smartphone to complete the transaction, dropping their merchandise into a white bag, which sales associates can easily spot to verify purchases before sending customers on their way. Shoppers who are new to Stance (and Moltin) will find signage throughout the store explaining the process of using the Moltin self-checkout system, if they are interested. Informational signage directs customers to "Skip the Line" and grab a white bag and fill it with merchandise. (The white bag acts as a point of differentiation; customers who are rung up by a Stance sales associate receive a black bag, clearly designating which checkout process customers are utilizing.)

Retail technology and in-store merchandising

Retailers are using in-store technology to help them make decisions regarding merchandising strategies.

Retailers can learn a lot about customers and the way they shop when customers connect with the brand digitally while in-store. Retailers have the opportunity to carefully monitor consumer response to their merchandising strategies to better understand sell-through, in-store navigation, and dwell time.

App, Wi-Fi, and GSM signals

Data acquired from usage of the store-branded apps provides retailers invaluable information. If a customer has the retailer's app, every time he or she visits the store, they are inviting the retailer to access information about their in-store activity. The mobile app allows the retailer to track customers' movements and follow them as they navigate the store. This impacts merchandising strategies as retailers are able to see where shoppers are spending the most time and what parts of the store may be underutilized.

If customers appear to be spending more time in a certain department, product, or product category, push notifications can be sent through the app. These notifications could offer a discount code or promotion, which might be exactly what the customer needs to incentivize them to make a purchase.

For customers shopping with a smartphone who have not downloaded the retailer's app, their movements can still be tracked through their mobile device. If shoppers are connected to the internet through free in-store Wi-Fi or their own private network, Wi-Fi and global system for mobile communications (GSM) signals can be collected by the retailer. These signals

5.12
Uniqlo ensures that shoppers know exactly how they can connect with the brand both during and after their shopping excursion. Tapping into the store's free Wi-Fi enables Uniqlo to collect GSM signals to understand their time spent in the store.

provide information about shopping behavior, including where, when, and how long customers spend throughout the store.

The data collected based on customer movements throughout the store can determine if there is a direct correlation between product placement and merchandise sales. It is important that not only are retailers collecting this information, but they are also analyzing it to improve both the customer experience and profitability.

Heat mapping

Retailers have the opportunity to carefully monitor, in real time, consumer response to their merchandising strategies to better understand sell-through, in-store navigation, and dwell time.

Monitoring merchandising strategies can be done through heat mapping; heat mapping allows retailers to better understand traffic flow within the store by tracking customer movements throughout the store. For example, a confusing store layout and/or experience makes it difficult for shoppers to find what they are looking for, and as a result, they will leave the store empty handed. By referencing the heat maps, retailers can make immediate adjustments.

Heat mapping uses existing store cameras to create a digital map, updated in real time through a dashboard, that shows how different parts of the store generate the interest from shoppers. The map uses various colors to show which fixtures, displays, and merchandise received the most attention from shoppers. (This is often referred to as **dwell time**, meaning what parts of the store customers slowed down or stopped in front of.) Heat mapping can zero in and tell retailers the exact item on a fixture that consumers paid the most attention to. This helps retailers identify effective product placement and fixture usage. By analyzing data from heat mapping, merchandising teams can better address opportunities for cross selling, suggestive selling, and effectiveness of promotional campaigns.

From a store planning perspective, heat mapping allows retailers to optimize store layout and functionality. By analyzing heat map data, merchandisers and store planning teams can identify dead zones, bottlenecks, and missed opportunities for customer engagement. Dead zones may be identified as prime real estate for in-store experiences; these same dead zones might encourage merchandising teams to feature more desirable products to subtly guide shoppers to these underutilized parts of the store. Areas that show increased traffic flow on the heat map might be remerchandised to call attention to undersold products or bigger ticket items as customers as these may not be sought after products.

The benefit to brick-and-mortar retailers is that, based on the information presented in the heat map, they have a clear picture of what is and isn't working within the store.

This information is incredibly valuable to retailers, especially merchandisers, for product placement and effective merchandising strategies. Fixture and merchandise placement is not static and can be moved at a moment's notice, so utilizing heat mapping to analyze traffic flow and dwell time allows merchandisers to make changes on an as-needed basis.

Buyers and merchandisers work together to analyze product placement to determine if product sell-through (or lack thereof) is the result of the product itself or its placement within a store. Sometimes all it takes is moving a product from one part of the store to another in order for it sell. This could mean moving product from a low-traffic area to a higher-traffic area; it could also mean remerchandising product so that complementary products are adjacent to one another as a suggestive selling tactic. Other times, it doesn't matter if the merchandise is featured in a window display, in an A (or gold) location within the store or featured in the marketing campaign; it simply isn't selling. This could be the result of an ill-timed trend or product offering, poor fit or quality, or a slew of other factors; at the end of the day, the product is likely to end up on the clearance rack.

If the use of and integration of digital technologies into brick-and-mortar stores is becoming commonplace (an expectation) for customers, why aren't these very technologies integrated into exterior displays? It can and should in order to attract unintentional shoppers. Chapter 7 will introduce the use of digital technologies in exterior store windows.

5.13
A mannequin grouping is an effective way to subtly guide shoppers to traditionally low traffic areas in a store, as mannequins are highly visible and act as a point of reference for product recommendations and styling advice.

Sustainability

Sustainable practices have been of increasing importance to customers in recent years. Not only are customers looking for sustainable apparel and accessories, but they are also looking to support sustainable brands. Shoppers seek information on sustainability and transparency as part of their brand research, applying it to not only the merchandise, but the retail processes as well. Visual merchandising initiatives need to address these customer demands through store design, signage, and in-store experiences.

Here are some steps that visual merchandisers can take to be more conscientious of the go-green movement:

1. Repurpose! Both from a budget and sustainability perspective, visual merchandising teams can repurpose props by using them in different departments and in-store locations, alter their appearance by adding paint or deconstructing the piece. Store planning teams can also repurpose in-store design elements.

    Follow The North Face's lead: The North Face opened a concept store in New York City's SoHo neighborhood that focused on sustainability. The messaging was clear as the store design incorporated repurposed materials such as reclaimed wood, steel, and granite, making a strong visual statement.

2. Utilize natural elements such as live plants and natural lighting. They create a warm, welcoming atmosphere. Green elements provide a quick energy boost for customers; natural lighting not only creates a pleasant in-store environment but also helps save energy costs.

3. Communication! Let shoppers know about your sustainability efforts! Tell them how you are reducing your brand's carbon footprint through signage, social media posts, and in-store directives.

Want to take it one step further? Highlight the positive impact your efforts have on the environment! Many customers today want their purchases to be positively tied to social and environmental causes; make it clear that their in-store purchase is tied to a greater good.

One way that retailers are working to reduce their carbon footprint and improve sustainability efforts is through printed materials found in-store, particularly in-store signage.

In Chapter 3 you were introduced to the Lush Lens app as the retailer began offering "naked" products (products without packaging) as a way to reduce wasteful packaging. Lush built this initiative out even further as they work to be more environmentally friendly throughout their brick-and-mortar stores, primarily by eliminating in-store signage. In 2019 at South by Southwest, a festival that integrates film, interactive media, and music, Lush piloted a store display sans signage. The seemingly simplistic display featured a colorized, linear display with the brand's fifty-four new bath bombs. What was noticeably missing was signage providing product information. Instead, attendees were encouraged to download and use the Lush Lens app to learn more about not just the bath bombs, but about Lush's push to go green. The app uses AI and machine learning to reduce brand packaging.

5.14
Banana Republic utilizes in-store signage to inform shoppers about sustainability efforts and product offerings.

American grocery chain Kroger has implemented sustainability efforts at store locations across the United States by eliminating paper shelf signage. Rather than providing product information printed on paper and displayed on store shelves, Kroger Edge is a digital shelf technology that eliminates paper shelf signage as well as reduces overhead lighting. The digital shelf technology provides product information digitally, which means illuminated messaging. As a result of the added illumination, stores are able to turn down overhead lighting to reduce energy costs.

Mannequins are also becoming more environmentally friendly as fiberglass mannequins are being replaced with more sustainable options. This is addressed in more detail in Chapter 6.

Company Spotlight: Sephora

Sephora has established themselves as a pioneer in omnichannel retail, providing a truly integrated shopping experience across their brick-and-mortar and digital platforms.

Sephora was founded in France in 1970 by Dominique Mandonnaud and became one of the beauty arms of LVMH Moet Hennessy Louis Vuitton in 1997. To date, there are over 2,300 stores in 33 countries, selling an array of beauty products, ranging from emerging to established brands, including Sephora's own SEPHORA COLLECTION. Since its inception, Sephora has been recognized for their innovative approach to the retail beauty industry.

From day one, Mandonnaud approached the retail beauty industry differently. Rather than keep beauty products behind counters and adhering to the "buy before you try" philosophy, Mandounnaud encouraged customers to test products before making a purchase. Products were not housed in counters manned by sales associates. Instead, products were easily accessible on counters and shelves, inviting customers to touch, smell, sample, and explore.

In recent years, Sephora has pioneered the omnichannel retail environment, coordinating efforts online and off-line to drive traffic and results on these complementary platforms. Well aware of the fact that their customers are using their smartphones while shopping brick-and-mortar stores, Sephora developed their own app to provide shoppers with a mobile experience catered toward their needs. The app connects shoppers with an array of in-store activities such as scanning product bar codes for product information, product reviews, and videos and tutorials. The in-store experience is highly integrated with the Sephora app and mobile devices, creating a digitally integrated, innovative brick-and-mortar retail environment.

Sephora has adopted the acronym ATAWAD as they work to provide limitless shopping "Any Time, Any Where on Any Device." They offer various mobile apps (Color Profile, My Sephora, Sephora Virtual Artist) that act as customized tools for customers to get personalized advice, learn about new product offerings, and provide a multi-channel shopping experience. The in-store experience provides interactive information centers, touchscreens, phone charging stations, a selfie mirror, and mobile pay in order to build customer relationships at what the company has named Sephora Flash stores.

Dubbed Sephora Flash boutiques, customers are able to shop the store's brick-and-mortar inventory as well as a digital catalog of more than 14,000 additional items. This catalog allows customers to add product to their virtual shopping cart, providing the opportunity for customers to purchase almost any cosmetics product they need from Sephora rather than shopping multiple retailers. They can pay for both their digital and physical purchases when checking out in the store, eliminating shipping fees that may occur. Customers shopping for fragrance utilize digital perfume testers, which means they can pick up a Near Field Communication tag for their desired scent, then scan it to learn more about the scent; the fragrance is then added to their digital shopping cart. Near Field Communication tags are used by retailers to transfer information to shoppers by pushing information to shopper's smartphones through small microchips (often found on stickers).

The phone charging stations and selfie mirror may take up valuable selling space, but the long-term benefit for customer engagement is well worth it. The charging stations in particular attract customers to the store who may have otherwise kept walking past the store. This is a valuable service to visitors, allowing them to pop in for a few minutes and charge their devices while browsing inventory they had not been seeking out. The selfie mirror provides an opportunity for shoppers to take photos of themselves as they test out new products, easily distributing it to their social networks for not only feedback, but also providing word of mouth advertising for Sephora.

How is Sephora engaging customers throughout their shopping experience? In select cities, the emphasis of the in-store experience is on the integration of digital technology and social media in the brick-and-mortar shopping experience. Shoppers are invited to engage with the brand through experiential retail, augmented reality, in-store tutorials, and Sephora's social media sites.

Here are a few examples:

Beauty Workshop Workstation

The Beauty Workshop Workstation is a set of twelve individual workstations where participants have access to live product, in-store iPads, and USB ports and Wi-Fi for customers who wish to use their own devices. The Beauty Workshop Workstation invites shoppers to explore all that Sephora has to offer, ranging from virtual beauty tutorials to live classes and product knowledge.

Sephora educators lead group beauty classes, inviting participants to follow the live tutorials or explore on their own using the iPads. Inspiration for new looks and skin and beauty solutions can be found on the brand's Beauty Board. Located adjacent to the Beauty Workshop Station, the Beauty Board is an oversized digital screen that features customer uploads; it is continually updated to showcase the different looks shared by Sephora customers.

Tap and Try

Placed as endcaps throughout the store, Tap and Try invites customers to choose any lip or lash product from the corresponding endcap and, through RFID scanning and Sephora's Virtual Artist technology, test out the different products. No messy make-up, no trying on and scrubbing off; just an opportunity to test out different colors and finishes with the click of a button.

5.15–5.17
A sneak peek inside a Sephora store's integrated technology. Shoppers are invited to immerse themselves in the various digital technologies throughout the store to educate themselves on how to use the different products sold on store shelves.

Company Spotlight:
Sephora, *continued*

Virtual Artist

Sephora's Virtual Artist provides users with the opportunity to explore any of Sephora's branded products by scrolling through and, with the touch of a screen, "try on" different looks and finishes. Users can test out foundation, blush, eye shadows, and lipsticks. When the user has finished their session, they can choose to have a photo message sent to themselves via SMS messaging or uploaded to their social media sites to share with their networks. By inviting participants to share images and product recommendations through their social media accounts, they have pushed information out to a new audience. In addition to the photo message, users also receive a comprehensive list of all products that were used during the session. This acts as a point of reference long after the visit to the store, reminding users about the really great products they found and encouraging additional sales.

Fragrance IQ

The purpose of the Fragrance IQ is to help customers find the best scent by inviting shoppers to find their custom scent match by completing a short quiz. After answering questions such as "Are you looking for fragrances that smell: anything, feminine, masculine?" and "Do you prefer fragrances that are: floral, fresh, warm and spicy, or earthy and woody?", fragrance recommendations are projected on the screen. Adjacent to the screen is a wall of fragrances available to test.

Users can also search the Fragrance IQ screen based on scent families, such as floral, fresh, warm and spicy, or earthy and woody. As shoppers learn more about the various scents, they also have the opportunity to read ratings and reviews, email themselves the fragrance information, and take home complimentary scent samples from Sephora.

Skincare IQ

Skincare IQ was created to help customers find the perfect products for their skin. The touchscreen asks users a series of questions to better understand what they are looking for. For example, users can search by skin concern, product type, product name, brand, or best sellers. After beginning their search process, additional questions are asked to provide more directed product recommendations. Product recommendations appear on screen and can be further categorized according to the type of skincare product. Each product includes detailed information about the product, including a product overview, list of ingredients, suggested usage, price, and user reviews. Once the user chooses which products they are interested

5.16

5.17

in, the Skincare IQ prints out the product recommendations and shoppers are directed to the product locations in-store. If shoppers are still unsure if they are ready to make a purchase, they can take home a sample of the product recommendations to test out before committing to a full-size product.

Pantone Color IQ

The Pantone Color IQ is a scanning system that analyzes a user's skin tone and suggests relevant products found in-store available for purchase.

How does it work? Sephora sales associates use a handheld color-o-meter and scan multiple parts of the customer's skin. They take the average of these different readings to determine the most accurate reading for skin color. Sephora customers then head over to the Color IQ touchscreen to find the products that are most relevant for them. Assigned a universal skin tone number, the Sephora sales associate inputs this number into the Color IQ database, which then recommends products that are found in-store that fit the users' skin match. Various filters can be applied for more efficient searching. For example, product recommendations can be filtered according to skin type, ingredients, coverage, and finish. If participants are short on time, they can click on the "email" link to have a complete list of the product recommendations sent directly to their inbox.

Sephora has also expanded in the subscription-retail arena, introducing Play! By Sephora boxes that integrate Spotify playlists into monthly beauty boxes mailed directly to subscribers' homes. "Integrating Spotify playlists into monthly beauty boxes will give Sephora a competitive edge by creating anticipation and consumer hype around its core product offering," said Laura Sossong, senior consultant at Boston Retail Partners, Boston. "Selecting the right music will further cultivate an emotional connection with the customer, elevating Sephora's perception and positively enriching the experience and relationship with the brand lifestyle."

The beauty boxes will also include mobile-specific offers and Play! Pass coupons to be used for in-store purchases, further integrating the users' shopping experience across various platforms.

Sephora has established themselves as a pioneer in omnichannel retail, providing a truly integrated shopping experience across their brick-and-mortar and digital platforms. However, the brand must continue to innovate; in what other ways can Sephora compete with other beauty retailers to ensure they are the go-to place for beauty needs?

Summary

As retailers work to draw customers into their brick-and-mortar stores, they are incorporating various strategies, ranging from in-store experiences to tech offerings to sustainability efforts. In several of the above examples, creative tech companies were hired for the digital installations. Perhaps visual merchandising teams will become a thing of the past or departments will become more integrated to incorporate varied skill sets. . . this would allow retailers to maintain consistency throughout omnichannel retail channels as well send targeted messages to customers. Next time you go shopping, look closely at the nature of interior and exterior displays. What experiences led you to the store? Kept you in the store? Excited you to talk to others about your shopping experience? These are important considerations for store interiors and building customer loyalty.

KEY TERMS

Computer vision
Dwell time
Heat mapping
Mass customization
Mobile checkout system
Multi-sensory experience
Point of purchase items
Sensing technology

CRITICAL THINKING: THE APPLICATION PROCESS

After completing the chapter readings, reflect on the information and experiences shared. Apply what you learned to future retail experiences:

1. Student Challenge: If the retailer offers both a mobile checkout process as well as a traditional checkout process, how can the sales team differentiate between shoppers using the third-party app and shoppers who will require assistance at the cash wrap?

2. Student Challenge Follow-up: Is offering different colored bags an effective way to subtly differentiate between the different checkout processes? Why or why not? Defend your position.

3. What products work best when utilizing sensing technologies, why?

Mannequins and forms

Overview

Retailers have been using mannequins and forms to show how merchandise fits on a body, but these visual merchandising display tools now have the capability to communicate directly with customers. By connecting with shoppers, mannequins and forms can make product recommendations, direct customers throughout the store, and provide valuable market research to retailers. In this chapter you will learn about the history of mannequins and forms before learning about the future of mannequins and forms in the retail environment.

6.1
Ralph Pucci: The Art of the Mannequin was an exhibit at the Museum of Art and Design (2015) that explored Ralph Pucci's innovative approach to mannequins and mannequin design. This image from the exhibit gives a behind the scenes look at how mannequins are created.

Communicating through mannequins and forms

Brands each have a unique story to tell; mannequins and forms are often used to bring the brand persona to life and connect with target consumers. Shoppers turn to store displays for inspiration in terms of seasonal trends, styling advice, and product availability. Using mannequins and forms within these displays enables shoppers to gauge fit of products and envision the garments on themselves and/or as part of their existing wardrobe. In simple terms, people buy what they see; featuring apparel and accessory items on mannequins and forms shows customers what to buy, rather than relying on sales associates to make the sale.

Many shoppers use the terms mannequins and forms interchangeably, but as an aspiring industry professional, it is imperative that you know the difference between these display tools.

Mannequins offer more structure than forms. Mannequins can be full-bodied, headless, or feature just one part of the body (i.e., legs only if you are emphasizing pants, socks, or even shoes). Oftentimes they are secured to bases using rods to hold them in place. However, not all mannequins use bases to stand upright; mannequins that stand upright on their own, without a base, are said to be "struck." Striking a mannequin means wrapping wire around the mannequin's waist and stretching it out to the sides until the wire is pulled taut, and nailing or screwing it to the floor as tightly as possible. The mannequin is then carefully balanced between the taut wires yet the wires are virtually invisible in the window (some window teams paint the wires so they disappear even more!).

6.2
An interior display comprised of a mannequin grouping and props at Bergdorf Goodman in New York educates and entertains shoppers, breaking up the monotony of the sales floor.

Additionally, not all mannequins stand vertically. Mannequins come in a variety of poses, including seated mannequins, mannequins that lay horizontally, active mannequins that appear to be in motion, mannequins leaning against a wall, and many more!

Dress and body forms are another alternative used by retailers to provide a three-dimensional shape to showcase merchandise.

6.3
An employee changes the shirt of a form used for display purposes inside a Pull & Bear store on Oxford Street in London.

They are softer to the touch as their bodies are padded, allowing for pins to be easily stuck into the body for draping and/or display purposes. These soft bodies stand atop a cast iron pole and four-wheeled base. Unlike mannequins, forms are not anatomically correct. Majority of forms do not have arms or legs nor do they have heads. For this reason, it can be more difficult to identify relevant merchandise to feature on the forms. For example, most forms cannot wear pants unless you purchase a full-body form.

In-store displays featuring mannequins and forms are just one way retailers are working to get consumers off their digital devices and shopping in stores. Mannequins and forms are used to showcase merchandise in a three-dimensional form; customers are able to see merchandise on a body, showing product fit and sizing, demonstrating hemlines, necklines, and sleeve length, as well as product details such as pleats and embellishments. Something that doesn't have much hanger appeal can be outfitted on a form or mannequin to allow shoppers to see the product on a body. The styling of mannequins and forms, both in structure and apparel choices, reflect the brand personality, product offering, and store aesthetic. Mannequins and forms act as salespeople as they make product recommendations, providing suggestive selling to customers without any directed, verbal communication.

For example, in 2014, Target dramatically shifted their in-store presentation to include mannequins in order to make the shopping experience even easier for their customers. As CityTarget stores opened throughout the United States, these smaller stores in urban locations acted as pilot stores for Target's new merchandising strategies. CityTarget stores were the first Target stores to include mannequins as part of the in-store displays for apparel. Prior to 2014, when shopping for apparel at any Target' location, customers were faced with a sea of fixtures. Customers who were short of time (and in reality, this describes most of the retailer's target customers), had to sift through one fixture after another, one aisle after another to see what merchandise was being offered. With the introduction of mannequins on the sales floor, Target found that within the first year, sales of items worn by mannequins increased by 30 percent. Mannequins truly provided suggestive selling as mannequins subtly provided outfit suggestions to busy shoppers. As customers filled carts with groceries, cosmetics, toys, and housewares, they could just as quickly grab head-to-toe looks for the entire family.

Before we look ahead to the future of mannequins and forms, it is helpful to understand their history.

Gowns courtesy of Pamella Roland

6.4
A.K. Rikks uses realistic mannequins in the Holiday 2018 window as an invitation to shoppers to explore a magical holiday shopping experience inside the store.

The history of mannequins

The earliest use of mannequins in the retail environment dates back to the late 1800s. **Mannequins** were first used to feature the newest clothing collections for wealthy customers. And, although in today's retail environment mannequins are still used to show the newest fashion trends, the overall look of mannequins has changed dramatically.

The first mannequins did not look much different from dress forms, aside from the materials used. The bodies were initially constructed from wax, wood, leather, wire, or papier-mâché and were simply headless bodies affixed onto iron bases. Some had limbs and were offered in three different poses: standing with both feet together or with one foot in front of the other; the arms were always simply hanging at their sides.

La Vigne was one of the first mannequin manufacturers to sell mannequins with faces, although these heads were outsourced to a mask-maker. The heads were comprised of papier-mâché and fitted onto the mannequin bodies. Other mannequin manufacturers followed suit, selling mannequin heads made from papier-mâché, wax, and plaster for a realistic look. These heads included glass eyes and wigs made from human hair.

Using wax allowed mannequin sculptors to be more detailed in their designs, creating more realistic facial features to connect with shoppers. However, the wax was not heat resistant, so the heat from the lighting used in store windows melted the mannequins, drawing in crowds for all the wrong reasons. Window dressers would complete a window, only to return the next day to see mannequins that had melted overnight! As a result, mannequin manufacturers began using papier-mâché and plaster for their mannequins.

After World War I, movable limbs were introduced on mannequins, creating displays

6.5
A day in the life of Grace, the Saks Fifth Avenue mannequin. Grace is carried to the basement to be fitted with latest fashion at Saks Fifth Avenue in New York.

that were more expressive by nature. Displays felt more realistic as mannequins and mannequin groups appeared to be more active as they were positioned to interact with one another. Additionally, mannequins began looking more realistic: necks became more elongated and the first mannequin with darker skin was introduced. Pierre Imans, a mannequin manufacturer, was the first to create a mannequin with darker skin tones.

In the 1940s, the first plastic mannequin was used in store windows. However, much like the wax mannequins of years past, the conditions within the window negatively impacted the mannequin itself. As a result of a chemical reaction in the window between the heat and the plastics, the plastic mannequins began turning green and had to be removed from the marketplace. Over time, the plastic mannequin was reworked and once again sold by various suppliers. However, these mannequins were heavy and difficult to maneuver around retail spaces.

Companies sought lighter and more durable mannequin alternatives, resulting in the introduction of fiberglass mannequins. By the 1960s, fiberglass mannequins became the industry standard; not much has changed today as fiberglass mannequins are still primarily used by retailers. Majority of mannequins used in the retail environment are made of white fiberglass; this allows the merchandise to really stand out when styled on the mannequin.

As mannequins play a role in supporting a retailer's brand identity, the overall look of the mannequin can be customized. Different finishes and mannequin details may be selected to ensure visual merchandising displays are on-brand. For example, in Uniqlo's New York City stores, store mannequins are translucent. When light hits the mannequins, they glow. These mannequins support the futuristic vibe of the store, as there are digital messages and bright lights found throughout the store. The lighting, mannequins, and store aesthetic complement one another.

Nordstrom, a Seattle-based specialty retailer, uses different colors and styles of mannequins throughout their stores. This is a fairly simple way for the retailer to differentiate one department from another. They recently commissioned mannequin manufacturer Ralph Pucci International to create thousands of gray mannequins with a raw fiberglass finish and exposed seams for one of their departments that sells trend-forward apparel for women. According to Pucci, Nordstrom wanted the mannequins to be very modern and edgy.

Retailers can customize more than just the body shape and overall finish. Within each collection, the various mannequin poses can be customized even further so no two mannequins are alike. Hair and make-up selections create entirely different looks to coincide with the retailer's brand aesthetic.

Mannequins can be realistic, abstract, or semi-realistic; they come in an array of poses, shapes, and sizes to reflect different activities and personalities. There are men's, women's, and children's mannequins; curvy, maternity, active, differently abled bodied mannequins. . . the list goes on and on. Some

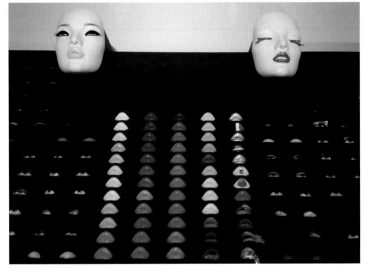

6.6 and 6.7
At the Goldsmith showroom, retailers can customize their mannequins by mixing and matching lip, eye, and lash color to vary the visual appearance of each mannequin.

mannequins are headless, some have sculpted hair, and still others require professional hair and make-up applications. **Realistic mannequins** have realistic facial features and wear wigs and make-up. In most cases, members of visual merchandising teams use theater make-up when applying make-up and styling the wigs used to create new looks on realistic mannequins. However, mannequin manufacturer Goldsmith created a collection for Christian Dior boutiques to simplify the make-up application process while promoting the brand's own cosmetic line. These newly designed mannequins use a magnetic system for make-up application on mannequins. This allows the visual merchandising team to easily apply and remove eye, lip, and nail treatments on the mannequins to reflect the brand's most recent makeup collections.

Some realistic mannequins are based off of well-known models, actors, or celebrities while others simply reflect the varied shapes, sizes, and able-bodied-ness of today's consumers. For example, Rootstein offers Twiggy and Beyoncé mannequins; Ralph Pucci has a Christy Turlington mannequin. When Kevin Arpino, one-time creative director of Rootstein, noticed a social trend of more curvaceous bodies like Jennifer Lopez and Beyoncé, he created a new collection inspired by this trend. Some male mannequins at Bergdorf Goodman have tattoos. Pro Infirmis, a German organization supporting the disabled, modeled a collection of mannequins that reflect people with a variety of disabilities. The collection included a mannequin with different leg lengths, a mannequin in a wheelchair, and a mannequin who has a spine malformation.

Mannequins are designed to reflect trends in body shape, current events, social trends, and shifting values. When there are new trends in terms of ideal body size, new mannequins are designed. For example, at the start of World War I in 1914, mannequins reflected the changing dynamics of women in the workforce. With men serving their country, the women at home began working in the factories. As a result, women were viewed as more practical assets in the marketplace.

6.8
Mannequins at the Derek Lam 10C Athleta launch party at the Athleta store in Soho showcase both the brand aesthetic and product functionality.

Mannequins reflected this change as waists were not as nipped in, hemlines were a bit higher and exposed the mannequin's knees and ankles, and bust sizes were reduced. Flash forward to the 1980s when at-home exercise videos were a trend; as a response to this trend, mannequins were designed with more realistic, toned features.

Mannequins are offered in an array of poses. These different poses are used to show personality, movement, and/or product capabilities; they also help set retailers and brands apart from their competitors. Some mannequins emulate runway models posing on the runway; others are sculpted in active poses depicting someone running, jumping, or stretching. Still more are based off of life interactions, inspired by people deep in conversation, grouped together for a photo op, or standing solo with hands in their pockets or arms folded across their chest. They can be standing upright or laying horizontal, leaning against a wall or sitting on a bench.

Athleta, an athletic apparel division of Gap Inc., uses mannequins that are based off the models used in their marketing campaigns; they "more accurately depict our strong, female customer," said Tess Roering, Athleta vice president of marketing and creative. These mannequins are in active poses that not only demonstrate the functionality of the garments, but also reflect the varied body sizes and shapes of the Athleta customer.

Some of the biggest names in the mannequin business include:

- Rootstein
- Goldsmith
- Universal Display
- Bonaveri
- Hans Boodt

The history of forms

Like mannequins, forms come in all different shapes and sizes. **Forms** were initially used for tailoring and dressmaking; they were behind-the-scenes elements used in the fashion design process. They are three-dimensional models of a body and are offered in different configurations. The most common form is the dress form, which represents a torso (shoulders to thighs). There are full-bodied forms that include arms and legs and there are dress forms with arms. There are men's, women's, and children's dress forms as well as special dress forms that include special sizes (plus size, petites) and forms based on physically challenged body shapes. The purpose of forms is to aid in the design process with patternmaking, draping, tailoring, and sewing. Placing a garment on the form allows the designer to see the fit of the garment, how it drapes, and how it would appear on one's body.

During the Industrial Revolution, retailers began using store windows for display purposes, so forms were brought out from back rooms and placed in windows as a selling tool. Dress forms were used to show the clothing options for sales within the store. We still see this today as retailers choose mannequins or forms for store displays depending on the brand aesthetic. Anthropologie, an American brand that targets creative, free-spirited women, uses forms rather than mannequins to display merchandise as it is more fitting for their feminine, soft brand aesthetic.

At the start of World War I, there were more changes for both dress forms and mannequins. With men serving their country, women took over their positions in the workforce. Mannequins and forms reflected the changing social trends as they were no longer focusing on the women's body, but rather what the women's body can do and/or accomplish in the workplace. Dress forms no longer featured corsets; instead, legs, knees, and ankles were highlighted.

6.9
A grouping of forms is used to create a casual, approachable presentation of coordinating apparel and accessories.

6.10
Soft-bodied forms allow merchandisers to easily pin apparel and accessories to the form to ensure fit as well as for display purposes. Forms may also feature varied fabric coverings to complement seasonal trends, store inventory, and/or brand aesthetic.

After WWI, the body shape of forms changed. The Victorian woman's body shape (large bust, small waist) was replaced by a more boyish body shape that was far less curvaceous, including a flatter chest. During this time, the materials used for forms and mannequins changed as well. At the beginning of the twentieth century, mannequins and forms were made of wax, but as a result of the Art Nouveau movement, dress forms and mannequins were then constructed from papier-mâché.

Today, there are dress forms designed for display purposes and dress forms for design purposes. Professional dress forms used in the design process stand atop a cast iron base with a pedal and wheels. The pedal is used to increase the height of the form to make the patternmaking, draping, and tailoring process easier. There is more padding on the body of professional dress forms than you would find on dress forms used strictly for display purposes. Dress forms used for display purposes may have cast iron bases, but others have simple stainless steel bases for easier transport. There are other forms that can be set on top of tables and shelving units and are considered tabletop forms. The bodies of dress forms are typically still made of papier-mâché and then are padded with layers of cotton with a linen overlay. In order to simplify the design process, the outer layer of professional dress forms are typically white, black, or another skin tone. Dress forms used for display purposes often have decorative exterior layers to create greater visual appeal. These can also be changed out on an as-needed basis to support seasonal trends and themes.

Some of the biggest names in dress forms include:

- Wolf forms
- Royal
- Modern Dress Form

The future of mannequins and forms

As we learned, the materials used for mannequins have evolved over the decades to make mannequins lighter, more durable, and less expensive. However, the evolution of mannequins in the retail environment will continue to be impacted by trends in the retail industry as a whole. As the retail environment is integrating more technology into brick-and-mortar stores, mannequins are evolving to include some of this same technology. There are a variety of ways digital technologies are incorporated in mannequins and forms, and we will continue to see this evolve. Newly designed mannequins may include touchscreens to inform, educate, and/or entertain shoppers.

Smart mannequins

In a 2016 interview with *Sportswear Magazine*, founder of French mannequin manufacturer Window Mannequins, Marc Mesguich, said that intelligent mannequins are the future of the fashion industry. Intelligent mannequins will help brands better understand their customers, allowing retailers to adjust their displays and merchandising techniques based on customer response, as learned from the intelligent mannequins.

Fast forward just a few years, and mannequins infused with computer technology are now available. Mannequins have evolved from static, fiberglass models to be more interactive components on the sales floor.

These **smart mannequins** allow customers to engage with the brand to learn more about product features that are of interest and/or relevant to their lifestyle and needs. Check out some ways that technology has become an important part of the design and function of mannequins:

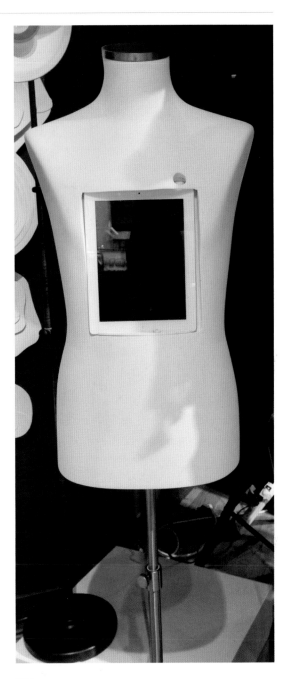

6.11
A tablet built into a form appeals to both the traditional and the tech-driven customer as a way to communicate additional messaging, connect via social media, and generate interest.

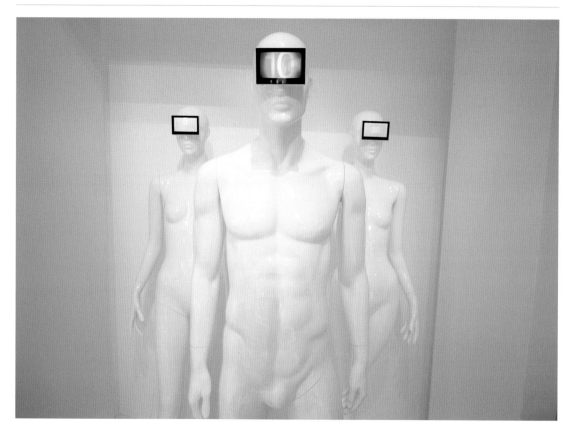

6.12
Are digital screens the future of mannequins? What type of information can be effectively shared?

- Scala is one company that has brought the smart mannequin to market. The mannequin looks just like a traditional mannequin, but the apparel worn includes sensors that are embedded in the clothing. Mannequins are positioned adjacent to a digital screen for information sharing. When a shopper activates the sensors in the mannequin's clothing, the adjacent screen highlights product content and capabilities, specific to the area of the clothing selected. By connecting with the smart mannequin, shoppers are in the driver's seat as they learn more about the brand, product specifications, and apparel highlights. The partnership between the mannequin and screen offers a seamless experience for shoppers to immerse themselves in both the tactile shopping experience that the brick-and-mortar customer craves alongside the digital integration that has become such an important part of consumers' lifestyle.

- Other mannequin manufacturers are integrating digital screens into the design of mannequin collections. French company Window Mannequins created a collection of mannequins that are equipped with digital screens. Atop the mannequin's face is a small digital screen, creating a futuristic appearance. These screens allow brands to communicate directly with customers, customizing messages, product recommendations, and promotional information.

- Nanasai, a Japanese mannequin manufacturer, has integrated artificial intelligence with their mannequin designs. In collaboration with Nextremer, Nanasai's innovative mannequins include artificial intelligence that allows the mannequins to speak with shoppers and respond to customer questions. The mannequin has a small camera embedded in its neck, capturing images of shoppers who slow down and take in the display. It uses facial recognition to gather and analyze data about the shopper. This is invaluable information for the retailers and brands as they can analyze the data to better understand their customers and create more targeted marketing initiatives.

- Yoshichu, another Japanese mannequin manufacturer, designed mobile mannequins. As the mannequins move around a store or display window, shoppers are able to see how clothing looks on a body in motion. There are small motors throughout the mannequin's body (most often in the neck, shoulders, elbows, and knees) that allow movement of the head, arms, and legs. Movements can be controlled via a remote control. For added entertainment, retailers may choose to display a group of Yoshichu mannequins to show interaction with one another or synchronize their movements for a high-impact display.

- Almax is another mannequin manufacturer that is utilizing digital technologies in mannequins. The technologies offered by Almax, however, are targeting the retailer as opposed to the customer. The EyeSee Mannequins by Almax have cameras embedded in their eyes to track the shopping habits of customers. Because the cameras are essentially at eye level with shoppers, they provide more detail about who is shopping the store than cameras that are typically found in the ceiling. Details such as age, gender, ethnicity, and dwell time can be tracked through the cameras. This allows retailers to gauge interest levels, traffic flow, and customer demographics to better inform their decisions, including merchandising strategies, marketing campaigns, and seasonal buys.

- i.Dummy is a robotic mannequin that changes in size right before your eyes. Initially created for designers, the i.Dummy adjusts to hundreds of different body measurements to represent an array of body shapes. Comprised of panels, the panels stretch and shift based on scanned body measurements. Although these mannequins were created with the design process in mind, they are beneficial to visual merchandisers as well for store displays. i.Dummy mannequins allow for retailers to feature an array of sizes and styles on one mannequin that can be moved throughout a store, potentially saving a retailer both space (storage of unused mannequins) and money.

Virtual mannequins

In addition to smart mannequins, we are also seeing **virtual mannequins** in the marketplace. As interior and exterior displays are incorporating virtual, augmented, and mixed realities, virtual mannequins are being introduced as variations of the traditional fiberglass mannequin. Virtual mannequins are digitized versions of physical mannequins. Retailers are using virtual mannequins to connect with shoppers in different ways as virtual mannequins have the ability to interact with customers.

Virtual mannequins not only model clothing, but they are also able to show clothing in motion. Virtual mannequins move around, allowing customers to see how the clothing moves on the body. Additionally, virtual mannequins can communicate with shoppers. They can be programmed to greet customers, direct customers within the store, and/or provide instructions to make the shopping experience more convenient. Virtual mannequins could include gender recognition, triggering the display images to change based on who is in close proximity.

For example, Macy's has tested virtual mannequins in departments targeting Millennials in a handful of their store

6.13
Fast Retailing's Gu Brand opened The GU Style Studio Store, where customers try on apparel and place orders online for later delivery. They also try out additional services such as playing with clothing combinations on a virtual mannequin and creating a digital avatar.

locations. How does a virtual mannequin work in a physical store? Oftentimes the virtual mannequins are projected on screens that stream recorded videos of models. The images are constantly changing to show a variety of looks that are relevant to the target customer. Rather than a traditional mannequin display that may be changed out on a weekly basis, virtual mannequins expose shoppers to an array of images, and as a result, a higher number of apparel and accessory options, in a short amount of time. An added bonus? The images are pre-recorded and display images can quickly be adapted based on weather conditions to create added relevancy for their shoppers. For example, during the sweltering summer months, models will be shown in swimwear, tank tops, and sundresses; an

unexpected rainy day will highlight wellies, raincoats, and umbrellas. Fall and winter displays incorporate more layering pieces. Additionally, these same images can be utilized across multiple store locations to create a more cohesive brand image.

Spanish fast fashion retailer Zara used virtual mannequins in 120 of their global flagship store windows in an entirely different way. Zara used window signage that read, "Shop the Look in Augmented Reality," trying to capture tech-savvy shoppers by directing them to download the brand's app. For two weeks, store windows appeared to feature simplistic signage ("Shop the Look in Augmented Reality"), devoid of mannequins or merchandise. However, if passersby were enticed to download and/or open the app, they saw something completely different. Instead of simple window signage, the window came to life throughout the app. Upon opening the app and pointing smartphones at the window, holographic virtual mannequins appeared through use of augmented reality. Virtual mannequins danced, posed, and interacted with one another to show a plethora of Zara merchandise moving throughout the screen from one location to the next. These movements allowed the user to view merchandise from all angles on human bodies. The virtual mannequins were Zara models who were photographed by sixty-eight cameras; as the models danced, posed, and talked with one another, their movements were captured from multiple angles.

If window shoppers liked what they saw in these AR infused windows, looks were easily shoppable and shareable via the user's mobile device. Zara created a one-click purchase option for shoppers to shop the head-to-toe looks; the app also included a tool to share the experience via social media (including selfies with the holograms!).

Headworks is another company that creates virtual mannequins. They have combined a 3D holographic head with a life-size mannequin to communicate with shoppers. These virtual mannequins are fully customizable and can say, do, and look however the retailer has chosen. The virtual mannequin incorporates RFID sensors, barcode scanners, image recognition, movement sensors, and facial recognition, allowing customers to engage with the mannequin, both for information gathering and entertainment. Shoppers and virtual mannequins have the ability to have conversations as responses to frequently asked, pre-recorded questions can be programmed in order to aid customers throughout their shopping excursion. The virtual mannequin also integrates beacons so smartphone users can use a mobile app to learn more about the products worn by the mannequin.

Lastly, retailers are also using virtual mannequins to create a more convenient try-on process for shoppers. Customers can create their own virtual mannequins (aka avatars) to virtually try on merchandise. Users upload a photo of themselves along with their height and weight and their avatar is created. Upon scanning a QR code, the avatar virtually tries on the garment, showing the garment in both a size smaller and a size larger for comparison purposes. Different colors highlight where the garment is too large or too small. This technology can reduce product returns as well as ensure fit accuracy for both online and in-store shoppers, creating a more efficient shopping experience.

TriMirror is one company that invites shoppers to create personalized avatars (virtual mannequins) to try on clothes in virtual dressing rooms. They have partnered with e-commerce retailer Jean Shop to offer virtual mannequins and virtual fitting rooms. Once shoppers find the product they are interested in, they are able to see it on a generic avatar. If the shopper would like to customize the avatar to more closely resemble their own body, shoppers can adjust measurements such as height, bust, waist, and hips, among others. In addition to body measurements, the virtual mannequin can be customized based on hairstyle, ethnicity, and style of shoe so that when "trying on" apparel, their own personal style is represented. When garments are tried on in the virtual fitting room, heat mapping is used on the mannequin's body to show how tight or loose a garment fits.

Body positivity and inclusivity

Throughout the fashion industry, there has been a movement toward body positivity, ranging from product accessibility to marketing and promotional messaging. People around the world are celebrating healthy, fit bodies (regardless of the numeric size) rather than seemingly one standard of beauty. The messaging is that consumers of all sizes and shapes should have access to fashionable

6.14
Seattle, Washington-based specialty retailer Nordstrom creates a focal point using mannequins of varying sizes and body shapes to promote size inclusivity.

favorably to the retailer's extended size range offered for the line. As a result, Nordstrom is pushing more of their vendors to increase the range of sizes they offer for their garments so the retailer can pass along these extended size ranges to their customers. The retailer has also altered their approach to mannequin displays on the sales floor as they are now incorporating mannequins ranging from size 2–16 throughout the sales floor, rather than only featuring plus-size mannequins in the corresponding department.

However, simply carrying these extended size ranges is not enough. With wider ranges of sizes offered on the sales floor, it is imperative that retailers utilize appropriate mannequins and forms to showcase the varied sizes. Retailers and brands are now integrating models and mannequins of varying sizes, shapes, and able-bodied-ness throughout marketing campaigns and store displays. Nordstrom, who is not new to offering special size apparel (plus size, petites, maternity), is now incorporating these mannequins throughout the sales floors. Rather than simply including these mannequins in their corresponding departments, a wider range of mannequins, ranging from size 2–16, can be found on display throughout Nordstrom stores. Albeit slow, the industry is shifting from unrealistic body shapes to celebrate the beauty of each and every person.

In 2019, NikeTown's London store featured an unexpected display of mannequins in their activewear apparel. Their newly revamped women's section featured curvy mannequins as well as mannequins with differing abilities in order to represent the range of body types of the Nike customer. A plus-size mannequin as well as a lower-leg amputee mannequin were prominently displayed in Nike apparel, reinforcing their brand messaging that athletes come in all different sizes, shapes, and abilities.

British fashion brand Missguided uses mannequins from diverse ethnic groups as well as mannequins with stretch marks, freckles, and vitiligo.

apparel, including the opportunity to see how garments will look on a body similar to theirs.

For example, when Nordstrom was interested in carrying the denim brand Good American in their stores, Good American was adamant that they would only sell the collection to Nordstrom if the retailer picked up the complete size range (00–24). Nordstrom agreed, and Nordstrom customers responded

The White Collection Bridal Boutique in Portishead, England, installed a window display that featured a mannequin in a wheelchair outfitted in a wedding dress. The simplistic window display was devoid of many props or other decorative elements but garnered a lot of attention because of the message of inclusivity.

We will continue to see retailers and brands embracing size inclusivity and body positivity. This will create a greater demand for mannequin manufacturers to increase size offerings for mannequins as well as the inclusion of differently-abled bodies throughout displays. According to Mesguich, there has already been an increase in demand for custom mannequins for retailer branding purposes. With the growing emphasis on body positivity, we will see an even greater push for custom mannequins as body positivity encompasses such an array of lifestyles.

Sustainability

Throughout the fashion industry, companies are focusing on the environmental impact of the decisions they make, be it manufacturing, logistics, or design elements (including store design). A component of store design, as you know, includes mannequins. Majority of mannequins in the marketplace are composed of fiberglass, which, unfortunately, is not very environmentally friendly, as it does not disintegrate. As a result, companies are seeking alternatives to fiberglass mannequins.

During London Fashion Week 2016, Italian mannequin manufacturer Bonaveri launched the first mannequin comprised of renewable, biodegradable materials. There were two primary challenges Bonaveri faced during the research and development process for designing sustainable mannequins. The first was identifying environmentally friendly materials to replace the plastics that are typically used found in mannequins; the second was improving the paints that are used during the finishing step. After years of research, Bonaveri developed two biodegradable materials that accomplished

what they were looking for. The first, BPlast is a biopolymer that is a natural, biodegradable material derived primarily from sugar cane. The next, BPaint, is a non-toxic paint finish comprised of 100 percent vegetable-based sources that are renewable and sustainable. Both BPlast and BPaint completely biodegrade at the end of their lifecycle, addressing the issue of waste management, making these mannequins full lifecycle certified. They also have potential to contribute to the reduction of CO_2 emissions released into the environment for each mannequin produced.

These BNatural by Bonaveri mannequins were first shown at the Green Carpet Challenge during the 2016 London Fashion Week. The event only incorporated materials that are either recycled or sustainably certified, drawing a lot of attention to the launch of these sustainable mannequins. Mannequins from the BNatural collection have been used by Stella McCartney and at the Salvatore Ferragamo Museum in Florence, Italy, among other retailers, museums, and special events.

Greneker is another mannequin manufacturer that is focusing on the environmental impact of the standard fiberglass mannequin. The GREN-S Soy mannequin is comprised of soy-based plastic for a more sustainable product.

Genesis Mannequins is a sustainable mannequin manufacturer, offering not only eco-friendly mannequins but also providing recycling services to reduce landfill waste. Genesis mannequins are comprised of organic, sustainable raw material rather than fiberglass. In addition to the sustainable components within the mannequin, Genesis Mannequins also include a finishing coat that protects mannequins from dirt and scratches; this increases the lifespan of the mannequins, in turn, reducing additions to landfills. When mannequins are damaged beyond repair, Genesis will dismantle and dispose of the various parts: metal inserts are melted down, the body is shredded and recycled, and the glass base is recycled.

Company Spotlight: Iconeme

The VMBeacon is installed directly into mannequins or other visual merchandising tools; it uses Bluetooth to transmit information to users via the Iconeme app.

Iconeme is a UK-based technology and design company that was the first to market with high-tech mannequins. These mannequins integrate beacon technologies into the mannequin design as well as other visual merchandising design elements.

Iconeme developed a VMBeacon that allows store windows and displays to communicate with customers about featured products. Shoppers are engaged in the visual merchandising displays as messages about product size, price, availability, and product location within the store are shared through a shopper's smartphone. Users can also discover what mannequins throughout the store are wearing, giving them instant access to an array of apparel and accessory items available for purchase. The VMBeacon is installed directly into mannequins or other visual merchandising tools (props, furniture, décor, etc.) and uses Bluetooth to transmit information (that has been programmed by the retailer) to users via the Iconeme app.

Shoppers who have the Iconeme app will receive an alert, notifying them that there is information to be shared. The VMBeacon then begins "talking" to customers, giving them detailed information about the merchandise they are looking at. This allows store windows and visual merchandising displays to communicate directly to customers, truly acting as the silent salesperson.

Brick-and-mortar retailers are competing with online shopping that is available twenty-four hours a day, seven days a week, oftentimes

making e-commerce a more convenient shopping experience. However, the VMBeacon draws customers back to brick and mortar retail by providing the ability for customers to gather information and make a purchase at their convenience, be it online or offline. The VMBeacon allows information to be transmitted before, during or after store hours; it can capture the unintentional shopper; or it can create an emotional connection with shoppers and entice shoppers to make a purchase in a quick and convenient manner. Shoppers are drawn to the beacon technologies because they are able to learn about the merchandise featured in store windows before taking the time to walk into a store and track down a sales associate.

The VMBeacon also allows shoppers to make a purchase, share information with family and friends through messenger and social media platforms, and save merchandise for later review and/or purchase. The VMBeacon also informs the user of other nearby offers and promotions available, creating a demand for shopping!

The VMBeacon creates and interactive and informative store display, allowing retailers to connect with customers and increase sales without customers having to enter the store. Store windows are visible twenty-four hours a day, seven days a week, but not always shoppable. The integration of VMBeacon invites customers to shop store windows, regardless of store hours.

British retailers House of Fraser, Hawes & Curtis, and Bentalls are among the first retailers to utilize Iconeme's VMBeacon.

6.15 and 6.16
When used alongside mannequins, VMBeacon allows users to learn more about the products they see on display simply by holding their mobile device in front of the display.

The VMBeacon allows users to see the various products that are on display, giving them the opportunity to add to directly to their shopping cart, download the image, or find out where the products are within the store.

Summary

The use of mannequins and forms on the sales floor is not new to visual merchandisers. However, as the retail environment is rapidly changing, mannequins and forms continue to evolve as well. The future of brick-and-mortar retail will continue to integrate mannequins and forms in varying capacities.

With an increase in digital technologies that connect shoppers and retailers, mannequins are becoming an important component to communicate brand messaging. This is done through both physical and virtual mannequins.

Additionally, as social trends such as body positivity and the go-green movement take precedence in the marketplace, mannequins and forms reflect these shifting dynamics.

KEY TERMS

Form
Intelligent (Smart) mannequin
Mannequin
Realistic mannequin
Virtual mannequin

CRITICAL THINKING: THE APPLICATION PROCESS

After completing the chapter readings,
reflect on the information and experiences
shared. Apply what you learned to future retail
experiences.

1. Research various mannequin poses; what
   are limitations that need to be considered
   when dressing the mannequins?
2. How do smart mannequins affect the store
   environment?
3. What are various ways smart mannequins
   can be used for both interior and exterior
   displays?
4. How might the use of smart mannequins
   impact both the front of house and back of
   house for retailers?

7

Exterior displays

Overview

Retailers are integrating digital technologies into exterior displays in order to educate and entertain shoppers. These interactive windows act as a point of differentiation between retailers and the static displays often found in retail windows. This chapter will look at the different ways retailers have connected with customers through interactive exterior displays, both through active and passive experiences for customers.

7.1
A mannequin named "Palette" moves its arms and head to strike a pose like a model to attract shoppers in a window of British men's fashion house Alfred Dunhill in Tokyo.

Interactive displays: Who, what, why

Window displays can be so much more than the static installations of years' past. As more and more shopping has gone by the way of online shopping, retailers can (and should) integrate these digital technologies into store windows to capture the attention of shoppers. The integration of digital technologies into exterior displays allows retailers to connect with and engage shoppers like never before, creating a new reason for shoppers to venture off the street and into the store.

Think back to your last visit to a brick-and-mortar store. What do you recall about that window display? My guess is there were a few mannequins or dress forms, some seasonal props, and signage calling out the designer, a store promotion, or product price point. Am I right? As you see, although there are brick-and-mortar retail stores selling just about any product you can imagine, the window displays rarely look much different from one retailer to the next.

In a highly competitive retail environment, engaging with customers allows retailers and shoppers to develop a relationship. Relationships are established through memorable, interactive experiences. For example, fast fashion retailer H&M created an

7.2
A digital window display features dancing Christmas characters on Oxford Street in London.

7.3
An advertisement fills the window of a Chinese clothing store. The oversized QR code targets the on-the-go customer and invites them to scan the QR code to learn about product offerings and events.

interactive experience that integrated the store exterior and interior as customers engaged with the brand.

Interior and exterior store displays should complement one another to reinforce brand messaging. At H&M's flagship Oxford Street store, not only did the interior and exterior environments complement one another, they actually influenced one another. H&M created an in-store experience in which the actions of participants directly affected the appearance of the exterior of the store. This experience kept customers running between the interior and exterior of the store to see the constantly changing displays.

In celebration of World Recycle Week, H&M projected a green coral reef in their windows and on the store façade; however, when shoppers inside the store walked across the sales floor, the colors in the coral reef in the windows changed colors. As a result, shoppers were responsible for changing the overall look of the store exterior. This kept shoppers engaged in the shopping experience, moving from store interior to exterior and back inside

again; the experience engaged shoppers as they were active participants in the store displays.

Oftentimes our first introduction to a store is the store window. Store windows are used to inform, educate, and entertain passersby; display teams use creative techniques in order to save both the sales person's and the shopper's time by making shopping effortless, providing consumers with information through visual mediums as well as suggestive selling. As retailers have increasing accessibility to digital technologies and shoppers are increasingly reliant on their phones, window displays no longer need to be static; retailers can (and should!) move beyond stationary mannequins, oversized graphic images, and printed signage.

These engaging store experiences attract and keep customers in their store longer, resulting in increased consumer spending. However, the biggest challenge brick-and-mortar retailers face is simply getting customers to walk into their stores. And shoppers no longer need to enter a store to be part of an engaging brand experience.

If you can't beat 'em, join 'em!

Rather than compete with the online shopping experience, brick-and-mortar retailers are now integrating digital components throughout the retail experience, giving shoppers a reason to visit brick-and-mortar stores as a complement to the online shopping experience.

When you see a store window, often times you want to know about the products featured in the window . . . what colors does it come in? Does it come in my size? Is my size in stock? Where in the store can I find it? Well, windows can respond to customer's requests and provide this information to shoppers; digital technologies can alert shoppers of product locations, prices, or inventory levels without stepping foot in the store. Interactive windows can engage customers by responding to their movements through motion-activated sensors, generating interest and creating an emotional connection. Or, interactive windows can simply act as an outlet for customers to not only shop, but also complete their purchase. As you can see, digital technologies can be used in various ways to entice customers to venture off the street and through the retailer's doors.

Conductive paint

Retailers are integrating digital technologies as a way for customers to glean additional information about a brand, product assortment, or brand history, among other things. As today's shoppers have information at their fingertips, retailers are using store windows as a way to pull shoppers in and differentiate themselves from competitors, oftentimes answering questions that shoppers didn't know they had. Shared information might include the history of the company or brand, manufacturing processes, social media pages, videos, and/or tutorials. Shoppers become informed consumers and feel connected to the brand.

Hiut Denim is an example of a brand that implemented an interactive window as a point of differentiation. As a small denim company competing with larger, established brands, they had to do something to create awareness and set themselves apart in a highly competitive space. They partnered with Knit, a creative tech company, to install an interactive display in the front window of Rivet & Hide, an independent retailer that carries Hiut Denim, among other denim lines. Since Rivet & Hide carries other premium denim lines, Hiut Denim did not want to simply use mannequins to show the denim on a body as it would be difficult for shoppers to discern Hiut Denim from the others found in-store. This interactive window created awareness of not just Hiut Denim's product offerings, but also the brand itself.

The focus of the display was a series of icons used to visually represent different topics that were of interest to consumers:

7.4
Interactive window displays create emotional connections between brands and customers, resulting in increased customer loyalty. Rivet & Hide featured an interactive window to connect shoppers to denim brand Hiut Denim.

Company Spotlight: Glass-Media

"The right message. . . at the right time, to the right audience. . . with the click of a button"

Glass-Media creates a truly seamless experience between the physical and digital retail experience. Omnichannel retail is a necessity in today's digitally connected world, but the brick-and-mortar presence is still an incredibly important part of the shopping experience. Glass-Media turns retail store windows into digital storefronts, turning the glass window itself into a screen for customizable digital messaging.

Digital messaging in store windows is not new, as retailers have utilized oversized screens to stream content and feature promotional messaging. However, Glass-Media projects content directly onto the store window, creating a more sophisticated and streamlined display.

These window displays can incorporate up-to-the-minute information, allowing brands and retailers to educate, entertain, and close the sale through the transformation of the physical storefront window.

Messaging is completely customizable and can be continually updated to address seasonal trends, promotions, and special events. For example, want to let customers read glowing 5-star product reviews? Feature them on your window in real time! Looking to connect in-store merchandise with runway looks? Stream the fashion shows on your window! Want customers to connect through SMS messages or a QR code? You guessed it. . . it can be done through Glass-Media.

How does it work?

Media is uploaded to the Glass-Media cloud and is projected onto a proprietary liquid crystal substrate that is applied directly onto existing glass. As a result, the projection can be featured in any size or shape that best fits the brand and their messaging. For example, a jewelry store may choose to use a cling designed in the shape of an oversized watch, using the face of the watch to display digital messaging.

Once installed, the retailer or brand has complete control of the projected messages using Glass-Media's browser-based content management system (CMS). The system is controlled remotely through an app or website, allowing the brand or retailer to upload and/or update content on an as-needed basis, including the ability to schedule their content playlist weeks or months in advance for seamless content streaming.

Glass-Media digital windows allow messaging to be featured on a single window or multiple store windows simultaneously for cohesive messaging. Additionally, if a brand or retailer has multiple locations that are targeting different customers, messages can be customized for each store location by using Glass-Media's segmentation tools. Display systems can be organized based on geographic location or ownership group, providing opportunities to vary the content for each location and/or target market.

Glass-Media enables store windows to provide engaging, interactive, and informative messaging, but does it turn window shoppers into buyers? Does it increase foot traffic to the store? Glass-Media's software programs also provide data and analytics to help brands and retailers determine effectiveness of campaigns. The software tracks mobile engagement through SMS and QR campaign activity, compares foot traffic to store sales to track conversion rates, and gathers data on foot traffic to map customer's path to purchase. This information is invaluable to brands and retailers as it allows them to understand, in real time, how their customers are shopping. This impacts product messaging and merchandising strategies to maximize sales.

What is the most effective way to truly immerse retail customers in a digital experience while shopping at a brick and mortar store? Perhaps it is creating be a shoppable site on the window, or featuring social media feeds, or even seasonal runway shows, or. . . or. . . or. . . the list goes on and on. In collaboration with Glass-Media, retailers can create customized content based on the needs of their target market.

7.5 and 7.6
The Fossil store turned oversized watches into digital screens to communicate with customers and push content to passersby.

brand history, product offering, factory, craftsmanship, and the denim itself. These icons were painted directly on the Rivet & Hide window using conductive paint so that each icon acted as a trigger point. When shoppers pressed their hands on the circular yellow icon, the triggers were activated; a light bulb lit up and the corresponding message was broadcast, connecting one's sense of sight, sound, and touch. Customers developed a better understanding of the brand and product craftsmanship, enticing them to step into the store and seek out Hiut Denim. For a small but growing brand, this was a way to create awareness and differentiate themselves in a competitive market. Simply by pressing one's hand to the window, users learned the history of Hiut Denim, different types of denim sold by the brand, and the manufacturing process.

Infrared sensors

Infrared sensors allow shoppers to interact with displays through motion. Motion activated sensors can be used in window displays as a way to entertain and engage with customers; as people pass by the window, products begin moving. These installations rely on a motion-tracking camera installed in the window along with motorized props. The camera tracks movements outside the window and triggers movement in the props based on the tracked movements. Passersby are engaged simply when walking past the window. The unexpected motion in the window creates a sense of surprise and excitement, resulting in increased attention given to the window.

For example, Lacoste used infrared sensors in a window display during Fashion Week 2013 to commemorate their eightieth anniversary as well as remind shoppers about Lacoste's involvement in the US Open. In the window of Lacoste's Fifth Avenue (New York City) store, tennis balls were suspended from the ceiling and the infrared sensors were installed so the tennis balls mimicked the motions detected outside the window. Passersby were "followed" by tennis balls as they walked past

the window. As shoppers passed from left to right or jumped up and down, the tennis balls followed. In addition to the motions, a soundtrack of racquets whacking a ball, bouncing tennis balls, and crowds ohhing and ahhing were heard outside the windows.

Whether participants were intentional shoppers or not, the active window display created awareness of the Lacoste brand, event sponsorship, and the store itself. The use of infrared sensors allowed shoppers to connect with the brand by creating a memorable experience.

Simple Human is another brand that used store windows to engage consumers through use of infrared sensors, but this time, infrared sensors were used as part of an interactive product demonstration. Simple Human sells home good products that help users operate more efficiently at home (think trash cans, soap dispensers, and shower caddies, to name a few). Simple Human products are sold at a variety of retailers, but at a higher price point than competing products. At Bed, Bath & Beyond, Simple Human wanted to justify the higher price point of their products and engage shoppers in what is typically a mundane purchase: garbage cans. The window display at Bed, Bath & Beyond utilized repetition and featured a series of oversized stainless steel garbage cans. As people passed by the window, the lids of the garbage cans popped open. Each lid opened one at a time, mimicking the customers' positioning. Once all the lids opened, the message "Have a Simple Day" was revealed. The purpose of this interactive display was not simply entertainment, but rather function. Simple Human showed users that they no longer have to touch the filthy lid on their garbage can when throwing their trash away. Simple Human garbage cans effortlessly utilize sensing technologies; disposing of garbage is as easy as simply waving your hand in front of the trashcan to activate the lid to pop open. The purpose of this installation was to highlight the convenience and ease of Simple Human products.

Levitation

Levitating products in store windows is a recent trend in store display that stops customers in their tracks. Floating products are unexpected, piquing curiosity in passersby. The key to integrating levitation in window display is the use of electromagnetic technology. The levitation base includes a floating magnet with a sensor; the corresponding magnet is affixed to the object that will be floating. The base can be masked within the display as long as the sensor is exposed. Products can float and/or spin without any type of support, garnering attention from unsuspecting shoppers. In the retail industry, levitating sneakers and jewelry are most often seen in displays, but the electromagnetic technology can be incorporated into just about any product.

Facial recognition

Facial recognition uses a camera and software program to first examine the physical features of a person's body and then analyze the data to determine age and gender. The camera might read one's face by calculating the distance between key points such as the eyes and the nose; another method is when the camera essentially reads the face as a topographical map. After the camera has completed reading one's face and/or body, the reading is analyzed. The software reports back on consumer behavior and shopper's interests based on the analysis, thus allowing targeted messages to be displayed for each customer.

Retailers are using facial recognition for one of two reasons: to customize messages or to interact with shoppers.

Facial recognition: customized signage
Think about your shopping experiences. Have you ever stood in front of a sign that has rotating messages? Ever notice that as you approach, the message changes to one that is more relevant to you as a consumer? Yep, you can thank facial recognition for that.

Retailers strive to cut through all the noise and create an integrated, relevant, and personalized shopping experience for customers. As retailers target a diverse set of customers with different needs, customized signage is used to create relevancy for different customers. Facial recognition is used to give marketers the ability to capture the characteristics of customers (age, race, gender) with a camera that uses an algorithm to analyze shoppers' faces to drive relevant messaging to the consumer. As cameras scan a customer's face, the facial analysis tells the retailer what customers in this demographic are interested in. The result? Signage that promotes products, services, and benefits based on target market profiling.

As shoppers approach the sign, the camera quickly scans their face and body, deciding which of the pre-selected messages are most appropriate. Using facial recognition, the signage will change to provide real-time information about products deemed to be of interest to the shopper.

However, there are privacy concerns with facial recognition. Because it is used in public places, there is no opt-in feature. Facial recognition operates at a distance, without the knowledge or consent of consumers. Another issue of concern is that facial recognition messaging can be biased. It has been shown that there is a higher rate of recognition for men than women; there is also a higher rate of recognition for individuals of non-white origin than for Caucasians.

To combat these customer concerns in-store, Mad Mobile Concierge introduced Hello Customer, which is a way for sales associates to connect directly with shoppers. Mad Mobile offers mobile retail technologies that help bridge the online and in-store shopping experiences. Hello Customer was created to combat the concerns of facial recognition. Hello Customer is used by retailers to learn more about who is in their store. Hello Customer notifies store associates when a customer has entered their store. Customers receive a text message welcoming them to the store while sales associates receive notifications with a customer's profile, including purchase history and shopping preferences. This type of information allows sales teams to tailor their approach to customers, providing a highly customized shopping experience.

Facial recognition: customer engagement

Facial recognition is also used as an opt-in experience to engage customers with the brand by inviting shoppers to knowingly participate in activities that rely on facial recognition. For example, retailer Jonathan Trumball used facial recognition to customize a story by including shoppers as participants in the story. Facial recognition allowed shoppers to be featured as a prominent part of the window. During the holiday season, the store's exterior window appeared to be minimal with a mounted LED screen with digitally enhanced falling snow, seemingly creating a festive, holiday scene. However, as shoppers approached the window, using facial recognition, the shoppers' face was scanned and it appeared in the LED screen

as a participant in a snowball fight. Shoppers watched the screen as they saw themselves get hit in the face with a virtual snowball. Images were posted to the retailer's social media sites and participants were invited to share their story on their social media sites as well. David Kingsley, Managing Director of Jonathan Trumball, said that the interactive window was used as a way to compete with online and mobile shopping. The experience "gave the in-store experience an edge and as a result, they saw a marked increase in shoppers," Kingsley said.

Virtual reality

Virtual reality (VR) uses computer-generated simulations to recreate environments or situations. In short, virtual reality is an artificial digital environment that completely replaces the real world. Users are immersed in this artificial digital world, allowing them to hear, see, and feel as if they are living in this world. Users wear headsets that stimulate their vision and hearing; their bodies' natural

7.7
Westfield introduces world-first Oculus Rift virtual reality headsets ahead of the immersive "Future Fashion" pop-up experience event.

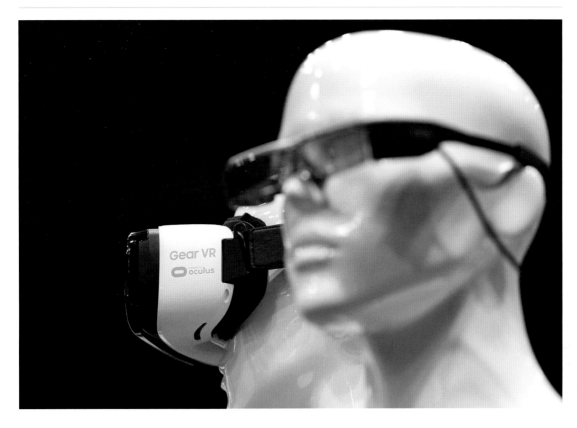

7.8
The Oculus Gear
VR Inc. virtual
reality headset.

reaction, be it moving in one direction or another, vibrating or shaking, makes users feel like they are completely immersed in a new environment. Users feel as if they are actually experiencing this new and/or different environment first-hand, yet they have not physically traveled anywhere.

To participate in virtual reality, there are PC-connected headsets and standalone headsets. PC-connected headsets connect to a computer or gaming console. They can be used in conjunction with other controllers, creating the most engaging virtual reality experience. The most popular PC-connected virtual reality headsets are HTC Vive, PlayStation VR, and Oculus Rift.

Standalone headsets rely on a smartphone or tablet screen to create the virtual reality experience. In order to use standalone headsets, users simply insert their smartphone into the headset to activate the virtual reality experience. Samsung Gear VR, Google Daydream, and Google Cardboard are

different types of standalone headsets. Other standalone headsets work completely on their own. Facebook's soon-to-be-released Oculus Go, for example, will not require either a computer or a smartphone to generate virtual experiences.

Virtual reality has been used by store merchandising teams to reimagine store layouts, traffic patterns, and obtain feedback from customers on products and store environment. Virtual reality is a much more cost-effective approach to making changes to store layout and design or the product development process. However, it is emerging in the way that retailers are using it to connect with customers as part of the store environment and merchandising application. Because virtual reality users wear headsets to create the virtual reality experience, users must opt-in to this experience and the retailer must provide the hardware and software to users. For this reason, virtual reality in store windows is challenging to use. . . but not impossible!

During London Fashion Week, Topshop utilized virtual reality in their flagship Oxford Circus store, transporting users to a front row seat at the London Fashion Week fashion show.

Rather than featuring Topshop merchandise in the store window, Topshop created a "Topshop Unique" window that featured the participants in virtual reality headsets and headphones, virtually experiencing the AW14 runway show as it happened. This generated a lot of attention, as passersby were curious and eager to participate. The window remained up for three additional days, connecting with a wider audience as it allowed shoppers to be part of the ever-popular, highly sought after Fashion Week experience.

Augmented reality

Augmented reality (AR), not to be confused with virtual reality, does not immerse users in a computer-generated environment, but rather uses one's existing reality as the foundation of the experience. Augmented reality layers computer-generated elements (such as images, videos, and games) on top of one's existing reality, creating an intersection between a virtual and physical world. In short, augmented reality is the overlay of digital content on the real-world environment.

Augmented reality is easier for users to interact with than virtual reality as users are operating in a familiar place, as it is their existing reality; they are not immersed in a new environment. Augmented reality incorporates apps and mobile devices to blend digital components into the real world in such a way that they enhance one another.

Augmented reality has been used by retailers to allow shoppers to visualize products in their own homes, "try on" products without stepping foot in a fitting room, or simply interact with a brand; it is a way to layer in images, both still and live, on top of the real world.

Ray Ban utilized augmented reality in a window to allow shoppers to try on glasses virtually to compare color, style, fit, and size simply by standing in front of the window. Users stood in front of the Ray Ban window, making sure their face lined up with the silhouette included on the screen. Once the software read the user's face, Ray Ban's product offerings appeared on the screen. The user could swipe through the glasses and as new glasses appeared, the user could reach up and drag the glasses onto their face, just as if they had physically picked up the pair and placed them on their face. At any point during this interaction, the shopper could click on the link that read "share the photo" and the screen was transformed into a Ray Ban photo op, providing a logoed image to be shared on social media to get feedback from their friends.

Just as we saw with virtual reality, augmented reality requires hardware to bring the augmented reality experience to life.

So how can you bring augmented reality experiences to life? There are two main ways.

Portable devices

Participants are able to use their own devices (smartphones, tablets) to activate augmented reality applications. Augmented reality apps rely on a user's camera to capture the real world and objects are then virtually integrated, allowing users to see them on the screen of their device.

Smart glasses and augmented reality headsets

Similar to virtual reality headsets, headsets and smart glasses can be used to create augmented reality experiences. Although the hardware may be similar, the output is different. Unlike virtual reality headsets, augmented reality glasses and headsets don't immerse users into virtual environments; they simply add digital objects to one's existing environment.

AdsReality creates augmented reality experiences for brands and retailers that allow customers to interact via their smartphone. The use of augmented reality in store windows (rather than something like an app or a QR code) creates a simple, convenient way for shoppers to engage with a brand. AdsReality's tech doesn't require customers to download

7.9
Fans interact with Star Wars character BB-9E on the Star Wars app. During Find the Force Friday II, the Star Wars app featured a global augmented reality treasure hunt at 20,000 retail locations around the world.

an app to interact with the screens, which removes barriers for customer participation.

This is important as the future of retail is about removing barriers to experience. Experiential retail is increasingly important, but it needs to be a seamless experience. A fast and frictionless experience will result in a stronger brand perception.

Consider this: you walk past a cool interactive display and it has caught your eye. In order to learn more, you need the retailer's app. Do you really want to fumble around on your phone, downloading their app, and completing the necessary steps to activate the interactive window? It is likely that your interest in the products and/or services featured in the window will quickly diminish with the various steps required to download the app.

Next, imagine you could simply hold up your phone to become part of the window. The ease and convenience of this frictionless experience increases the relationship between the user and the brand.

Mixed reality

Now that you know the difference between virtual reality and augmented reality, it's time to take a closer look at **mixed reality (MR)**, sometimes called hybrid reality. Mixed reality enables users to immerse themselves in the world around them AND interact with a virtual environment simultaneously. There are two different types of mixed reality: one in which participants engage in a reality that is built upon their actual environment OR a mixed reality in which participants engage in a reality that is rooted in a virtual reality. In mixed reality, virtual content is found as an overlay on the real environment (as in AR) but it also interacts with one's real environment.

For the first example, put simply, users can see virtual objects just like they would in augmented reality, but these objects can also interact with the real world. In a sense, mixed reality is a more immersive and interactive type of augmented reality. In this case, a user remains in the real-world environment while digital content is added to it. This form of mixed reality can be considered an advanced form of augmented reality. The Holographic devices like Microsoft Hololens are used in this type of mixed reality experience. These headsets have translucent glasses that allow users to perfectly see their surroundings. Virtual experiences are created with the help of holograms.

In the second type of mixed reality, users see and interact with a completely virtual environment that is seen as an overlay on the real world around them; digital objects overlap objects that exist in one's actual environment. Participants use a headset to track their actual environment, enabling the virtual environment to be updated and adjusted according to what has been "read" through the headset. This kind of mixed reality is closer to virtual reality than augmented reality; in fact, some virtual reality headsets have sensors to track the physical environment too. These headsets have non-translucent displays that completely block out the real world (just like virtual reality headsets) and use cameras for tracking. Windows mixed reality headsets are used for this type of experience.

Toms Shoes incorporated a really great example of mixed reality, placing virtual reality headsets into 100 stores, enabling the brand to virtually transport customers to Peru to see the impact of their "One for One" giving campaign on local people.

Imagine this:

You visit your favorite retailer, eager to buy a pair of Toms Shoes. You know the deal: buy a pair for yourself, and a pair is given to someone in need. This is a business model we are seeing more and more of.

Now, imagine you step into the life of that "someone in need." You put on the Hololens and you are immediately taken to another world; as you turn your head to the left and to the right, it is a desolate land. Abodes. Dirt floors. Not a shopping mall or sign of commerce around. You walk through the village as locals smile and wave at you. Suddenly, you know what is like to be a person in need; the notion of who/what/where your donation is going is now

so real. You realize that buying a pair of Tom's Shoes is a small way to make a difference in the lives of those who need it most. You are sold; Tom's Shoes has a customer for life.

Not only did this improve awareness of their social corporate responsibility and promote their giving campaign, it also gave customers an unforgettable and immersive experience they were unlikely to forget. The Hololens created a powerful message that cannot be replicated through storytelling; it is about the experience.

Extended reality

Extended reality, also known as cross reality, is, more or less, all encompassing of augmented reality, virtual reality, and mixed reality. It refers to the real and virtual environments generated by computer graphics and wearables.

This means that in extended reality, existing and virtual imageries co-exist and work across various platforms. Extended reality enables interactions in virtual realities. This will become incredibly valuable both for connecting with customers and building a robust business. Extended reality will be used as part of e-commerce platforms and enhancing the self-service retail environment; from a business perspective, extended reality will be used for design applications as well as for operations, training and development, and providing consumer insights.

Mobile commerce

Mobile commerce (m-commerce) is the process of buying and selling products and services through the use of internet and cellular data on devices such as cell phones, iPads, and tablets. Although consumers are spending a lot of time online on their mobile devices, few are actually using their mobile devices to make a purchase. Sixty percent of online traffic is through mobile devices, yet only 16 percent of internet purchases are done on mobile devices. Retailers are trying to convert mobile shoppers into buying customers; they are doing this by integrating store windows into shoppers' mobile devices, getting customers to look up from their phones and utilize interactive technologies that are front and center in store windows. Take a look at how retailers are tapping into mobile devices to connect with shoppers, create awareness, and drive sales.

As part of a Father's Day promotion, Bloomingdales and Ralph Lauren partnered to install interactive window displays to convert passersby into paying customers. Together, the two brands transformed six windows of Bloomingdale's flagship location in New York City into a touchscreen where shoppers on-the-go could browse, personalize product, checkout, and walk away with a full shopping bag without ever stepping foot in the store or talking to a sales associate. How did they do it? They turned store windows into shoppable sites!

Shoppers could browse color swatches on a touchscreen, determine the apparel or accessory item (shirt, tie, or pants), and color choice, and see their customized product brought to life on the screen in the window. If shoppers decided to purchase their designs, all they had to do was text POLO for a link to checkout. A sales associate would then hand-deliver the merchandise to the customer on the sidewalk.

"We wanted to create an interactive experience that would literally make you stop in your tracks with something theatrical and mesmerizing," said David Lauren, Ralph Lauren's Executive Vice President of global advertising, marketing, and corporate communications.

Kate Spade, a bridge contemporary brand best known for her colorful graphic prints and playful sophistication, also took advantage of the "silent salesperson" as they converted a storefront window into a direct-to-consumer selling opportunity. As the brand was building out a retail space for the new line Saturday, they turned the window into an oversized iPad displaying the Kate Spade Saturday e-commerce site. Selling apparel, jewelry, handbags, and shoes, the goal was to attract shoppers to the brand as they were building out a pop-up shop for the line. Kate Spade captured shoppers when the line

Saturday was in its infancy, and before the store was open, by providing a shoppable site; curious shoppers were converted into paying customers right then and there. After filling their virtual shopping cart, the checkout process required users to enter their mobile number. A text message was then

7.10
Online shoppers continue holiday spending on Cyber Monday: George Wade tries "cyber shopping" with an interactive window display outside the Ralph Lauren store along the Magnificent Mile shopping district in Chicago, Illinois. The window allows shoppers to order Ralph Lauren's merchandise by simply touching the window display.

sent to complete the order and arrange for merchandise delivery. In some areas, orders were delivered to customers within an hour.

Unlike other tech-driven windows, these windows created a shoppable experience, selling jewelry, apparel, and shoes directly to customers: customers were invited to interact not just with technology, but also with the merchandise. By engaging with customers, retailers are creating an emotional relationship with users. The added convenience and novelty of hand-delivered merchandise and one-hour delivery set these branded experiences apart in the era of instant gratification.

Social media

Companies are spending a lot of money to connect with social media users. Integrating social media in store windows across communities, in varied locations, encourages content sharing. This, in turn, increases the visibility and impact of the display.

In fact, it was predicted that in 2019, advertisers would spend nearly $84 billion USD globally advertising on social media (Gesenhues, 2019). However, according to Nielsen, 92 percent of consumers believe recommendations from friends and family over all forms of advertising. So, rather than spend money advertising on social media, retailers are turning to customers for content generation in order to create awareness of their brand on social media. User-generated content is more effective than brand-generated content.

One way in which user-generated content is created is through subtle invitations for in-store participation. This is done through digital stories and/or backdrops, inviting shoppers to star in the story and share it with their social networks. These stories become collaborative; participants feel like they played an active role in the storytelling process and the retailer set the stage for participants, ensuring that they don't have to look too hard for their social media moment. The stories are then shared on social media, promoting the retailer to the hundreds, if not thousands, of potential customers through social media networks.

For example, when promoting the launch of their Tease perfume line, Victoria's Secret designed the store windows with selfies in mind, knowing that not only is the Victoria's Secret customer constantly taking selfies, but also that these selfies are shared on social media. The window, and marketing campaign, asked shoppers to take a selfie with the window as the backdrop and post it to their social media sites, tagging the photos with #VSTease and #VSGift; each post that included the hashtags was eligible for a surprise gift (Tease perfume roller). This simple tactic garnered nearly 2,000 selfies of shoppers in front of the Victoria's Secret window. The return on investment for Victoria's Secret was huge, as 70 percent of customers are finding out about a product outside of the brand's advertising. These selfies acted as free marketing for Victoria's Secret, casting a wide net by tapping into the social networks of their existing customers.

Macy's American Icons campaign that benefits American veterans and their families relied on user-generated content on their social media feed to drive awareness of not just Macy's products, but the heroism of members of the armed forces. Macy's customers were invited to tag and share selfies on social media outlets for a chance to win a prize. The word-of-mouth marketing increased awareness of Macy's, the featured brands, and the American Icons campaign. Tagged images were displayed in store windows on a digital screen to show Macy's product on actual customers. Additionally, store windows featured window signage that outlined the process for participation in the American Icons campaign alongside mannequins and the digital screens.

Social media and mass customization

Integrating social media into digital window displays for customization opportunities is another way retailers are inviting shoppers to be a part of the overall window design. Another example of social media usage in retail windows was found during holiday 2013 windows at Saks Fifth Avenue. Saks invited shoppers to participate in the design of their Fifth Avenue storefront window by using social media and mass customization to engage customers in the design process.

Mass customization, as introduced in Chapter 5, allows retailers to offer a limited menu of options for users to customize products or services. In the case of the Saks window, shoppers could design a snowflake based on pre-existing design options within the software program.

The Yeti-themed window invited customers to visit the Saks website, use mass customization to design a snowflake, then watch the snowflake(s) (along with their name) trickle down the Saks Fifth Avenue window. The window was filled with customized snowflakes as shoppers often designed several snowflakes; they then snapped selfies and posted the images to social media, notifying their network of contacts. This word-of-mouth advertising generated awareness of the Saks Fifth Avenue brand, directed viewers to the Saks website to customize their own snowflake or to the brick-and-mortar store to customize a snowflake, and see it featured in the window. After seeing the customized snowflakes fill the window, shoppers were able to get a 3D printed snowflake in the store, which helped Saks bring window shoppers into the store, knowing that once a shopper enters a store, they are more likely to make a purchase, whether it is a planned, impulse, or complementary purchase. As Saks customers awaited their 3D printed snowflake, they were exposed to an array of products for sale to help them complete their holiday shopping.

7.11
The Saks Fifth Avenue in New York City encouraged window shoppers to be part of the overall window design by creating their own snowflake. Participants were able to see their name and snowflake trickle down the window for their fifteen minutes of fame.

Company Spotlight: WindowsWear

WindowsWear's database has over 250,000 images of store windows, interior displays, creative news and information, and e-commerce packaging videos and more. It is THE place to find inspiration for fashion displays, ranging from historic to real-time installations.

WindowsWear provides users access to the world's largest digital archive of fashion window displays. The subscription-based database highlights window displays across the globe, dating back to 1931. Mike Niemtzow, Jon Harari, and Raul Tovar founded WindowsWear in 2012.

Mike was walking to work one day when he came across Anthropologie store window displays that stopped him in his tracks. He was in awe of the amazing combination of fashion and art and realized that access to visual merchandising displays was limited, not only on a national scale, but globally as well. Mike is constantly looking for ways to reinvent and bring a new perspective to the things we experience and see in our everyday lives, and this ah-ha moment inspired him to want to make images of store windows accessible for people worldwide.

Today, WindowsWear is the leading visual design resource used by top brands, designers, and educational fashion programs worldwide. WindowsWear provides its users access to a database of over 250,000 images of store windows, interior displays, creative news and information, and e-commerce packaging videos and more. The best known brands in the industry such as Coach, Tory Burch, Marc Jacobs, Ralph Lauren, to name a few, use WindowsWear. In addition, many visual merchandising teams, architects, designers, and schools subscribe as it is the only digital database of its kind that provides digital imagery and current industry news focused on the various facets of visual merchandising. WindowsWear is THE place to find inspiration for fashion displays, ranging from historic to real-time installations.

In order to bring the digital database to life, WindowsWear provides off-line experiences as well.

In 2013, WindowsWear launched WindowsWear Fashion Window Walking Tours and WindowsWear Workshops and in 2016, the WindowsWear Museum opened.

WindowsWear Fashion Window Walking Tours

The Fashion Window Walking Tours provide participants access to some of New York City's best visual merchandising displays, including both interior and exterior installations. Participants are guided through the city, taking in the city's flagship stores, ranging from department stores to boutiques and innovative design studios. Throughout the tour, participants learn the ins and outs of how the different fashion displays are created.

In addition to seeing some of the most iconic retailers and brands, the tour provides information about seasonal trends, the design process, and background information about some of the most iconic fashion brands. Talk about window-shopping!

WindowsWear Workshop

Led by Eric Feigenbaum, a recognized leader in visual merchandising and store design with over 30 years of experience, the WindowsWear Workshop teaches store owners, brands, entrepreneurs, and aspiring industry professionals how to use visual communication and holistic design to engage customers and maximize sales. The two-day workshop incorporates discussions and a "NYC Retail Safari" that brings the classroom discussions to life through retail visits throughout the city. The Retail Safari allows workshop attendees to see how best practices are implemented in the marketplace by an array of retailers and brand houses.

WindowsWear Museum

The WindowsWear Museum is the world's first museum of fashion windows and in-store displays. Housed at Berkeley College, the museum activates the digital images through installations executed by some of the biggest names in the fashion industry. The museum exhibits rotate continually and highlight different

7.12
Fendi window in New York City, July of 2014.

brands and retailers. Each installation includes information about the people and their vision that brought it to life. The museum's opening coincided with Coach's 75th anniversary, and the inaugural installation was executed by Coach's designers and production teams to pay homage to the brand's historic ties to New York. The installation featured a New York City subway car infused with Coach products throughout the car. The installation also featured replications of Coach's vintage advertisements, allowing guests to experience the evolution of the brand.

WindowsWear professional development conferences

In 2019, WindowsWear launched its three-day teacher professional development conference. Its purpose is to develop family and consumer science, design, merchandising, and fashion teachers with the latest thought leadership in creativity, design-thinking, and technology, by experts in fashion, interior design, business, and merchandising in New York City. Educators

spend three event-filled days in New York City engaging with leaders in fashion, visuals, and creative. The schedule includes in-class instruction, showroom visits, a Broadway show with a backstage tour, social events, and much more.

WindowsWear Student Awards

The inaugural annual WindowsWear Student Awards was launched in May of 2019. Schools and their students upload pictures and videos of their best work to their WindowsWear profile. WindowsWear then selects nominees across more than ten categories such as best branding, best interior design concept, best window display, and much more. WindowsWear members and nominees are invited to the WindowsWear Student Awards held in NYC each May where the winners are announced. In 2019, WindowsWear awarded more than $5,000 in cash scholarships. Be sure to submit your work by April for your chance to win a cash scholarship!

Summary

As you can see, innovative technologies allow for improved customer engagement, helping to not only connect shoppers and retailers, but also create a seamless shopping experience. As retailers struggle to get customers into brick-and-mortar stores, increased customer engagement creates a point of differentiation. Rather than waiting for shoppers to venture through the doors of their favorite brick-and-mortar stores for experiential retail, retailers can engage customers through digitally integrated external displays. This chapter introduced ways that retailers are engaging customers, but as new technologies are introduced, retailers must continue to evolve as well.

KEY TERMS

Augmented reality
Facial recognition
Infrared sensors
M-commerce
Mixed reality
Virtual reality

CRITICAL THINKING: THE APPLICATION PROCESS

After completing the chapter readings, reflect on the information and experiences shared. Apply what you learned to future retail experiences:

1. The chapter reading includes examples of interactive store windows; research others that have been done and/or propose your own idea of a digitally connected store window.

2. Upon reviewing the examples of interactive store windows provided in Chapter 7, how might these store windows include one additional step to close the sale with their captive audience?

3. Create an AR/VR experience for shoppers; what story are you trying to tell? What experience have you created?

Conclusion

Throughout this text, we focused on the successes in the marketplace pertaining to the integration of digital technologies in brick-and-mortar shopping. However, for every success story, there are many retail experiences that don't quite hit the mark, retail experiences in which, for some reason, the customer buy-in was not there. There are a multitude of reasons why new experiences don't work out. Perhaps the technology was too cumbersome; or it was not relevant for the retailer's target market. Perhaps the technology was introduced too early and customers just didn't get it. It was in a poor location; it wasn't user friendly. . . the list goes on and on.

ShopWithMe is one such retailer that integrated digital technologies throughout the brick-and-mortar shopping experience, but the store that was once dubbed "the future of retail" never quite took off.

Launching during holiday 2015 in Chicago, the ShopWithMe store represented a new type of pop-up shop. ShopWithMe was part store, part tech pod.

In short, the concept of ShopWithMe was a traveling pop-up shop integrated with high-tech solutions to retail logistics. The goal? An easy-to-build/easy-to-break down, completely mobile store designed to be mass-produced for future iterations in locations all over the world.

The first iteration housed collections from Toms Shoes and Raven + Lily. The interior utilized smart fixtures such as glass top digital displays, touchscreens, and virtual reality to communicate with shoppers. These displays allowed customers to learn more about the merchandise, receive product recommendations based on what they were browsing while in-store, and/or complete their purchase. As customers walked past the walls, shelves on the wall moved toward the shopper as a way to recommend items.

All products and fixtures were RFID-embedded, and the store included beacons so that customers with the ShopWithMe app received product suggestions and personalized messages. While in-store, the technology offered endless aisles as shoppers also had the ability to scan items to find more options, request items to try on, build a cart and check out. Many of these elements have been discussed throughout the text. The technology has proven to be successful, but you likely have not heard of the ShopWithMe store itself.

So, where is ShopWithMe today? Unfortunately, the ShopWithMe model never moved beyond its short stint in Chicago. How did one of Nevada's most well funded start-ups gain so much traction and then fail to deliver? Where did they go wrong?

Another retailer reinventing the pop-up store through integration of digital technologies is Showfields. However, Showfields' integration of digital technologies is focused more on the products and less on the retail processes.

Showfields is a reimagined department store offering digitally native brands a brick-and-mortar space to activate their products; Showfields is about more than just selling merchandise. Showfields was conceptualized as an immersive retail space, combining short-term pop-up shops with art exhibitions, theater, and community events. Because the brick-and-mortar space is built out as a modular system, each brand has it's own platform to activate products and experiences. Brands can either focus on the pop-up showroom space, be incorporated in the House of Showfields theatre space, or a combination of the two. These approaches provide customers the opportunity to engage their senses throughout the shopping excursion. When the brand's four or six month rotation wraps, a new Instragram-favorite brand moves in and the space becomes unrecognizable, yet again. According to one of Showfields' founders, Tal Zvi Nathanel, "It's a plug-and-play model for brands. Our team gives the brand the whole experience from design and build and they get an opportunity to push forward and optimize their relationship with the customers walking in the door" (Danziger, 2019).

Showfields opened their doors in New York in December 2018 and have additional locations in the works.

As you see with the ShopWithMe example, the infusion of technology in the retail environment does not ensure a successful retail venture. Retailers both large and small can utilize retail technologies to improve the customer experience in various ways. There are much smaller brick-and-mortar retailers that have remained relevant alongside the likes of retail behemoths Amazon and WalMart; budgets may be smaller, but the execution within the retail environment is spot-on. The tech is relevant and timely for the retailer's target market.

What is on the horizon for the integration of digital technologies in the brick-and-mortar retail environment?

In 2020, the buzzword is 5G. This refers to the network connectivity, meaning 5G is the fifth generation for network connectivity. To give you a little background on network connectivity and what we have come to expect:

According to ORDRE, a fashion company that integrates fashion and new technologies, "First generation (1G) networking brought mobility to phone calls; 2G enabled short text messaging; 3G provided essential networking speeds for smartphones; and 4G gave rise to deep web functionality and the launch of mobile commerce. Now, the world is on the cusp of a new wireless era with the onset of fifth generation (5G) connectivity."

Why is this relevant for the physical shopping environment? As we discussed throughout the text, the brick-and-mortar shopping environment is full of opportunities for the integration of retail technologies. These technologies enable retailers, brands, and customers to communicate with one another in real time. One thing retailers have learned through the integration of digital technologies is that speed matters. The use of 5G will allow brands and shoppers instant access to one another, reinforcing the instant gratification mentality we have come to expect. The faster customers are able to connect with brands, be it through a form of e-commerce (e-commerce, s-commerce, or m-commerce), product customization, or gaining product knowledge, the more money shoppers will spend with said retailer. From a business perspective, the faster brands receive information about customers, the more personalized product and service offerings can be.

This 5G technology will improve the speed of facial recognition, product recommendations, and frictionless payment options. We might see more customizable products, the use of drones for product deliveries, smart fitting rooms, and virtual reality/augmented reality/mixed reality experiences.

However, as new technologies are developed, there is no question they will be integrated into the nearly thirty trillion-dollar retail industry. It is a matter of when and how, not if. It is an exciting place to be. . . **make it happen**!

Glossary

Accent lighting: light source within a store used to create visual interest

Ambient lighting: main light source in-store, providing bright enough light to see the merchandise

Americans with Disabilities Compliant signage: (ADA) signage used to inform customers that the shopping environment is accessible to all customers

Augmented reality: uses computer-generated elements within one's existing reality

Beacon technologies: small wireless devices that transmit signals to an app via Bluetooth

Brand-generated content: component of marketing strategy in which the retailer or brand creates content to be shared with consumers

Brand storytelling: marketing tactic in which retailer uses a narrative (story) about the brand to connect the brand, their mission, and/or values to the customer

Computer vision: computers act like humans; computers identify and interpret information from images and 3-dimensionally and then take action of some sort (make product recommendations, etc.)

Connected fitting room: also known as smart fitting room or interactive fitting room; allow customers to communicate directly with store associates and websites to simplify the fitting room experience

Conversational commerce: a form of e-commerce that is done via speech recognition

Custom fixtures: fixtures that are customized for a specific client; will not be found elsewhere

Customizable lighting: in-store lighting that allows the shopper to adjust the lighting to best depict time of day and/or occasion the products will be worn

Decorative lighting: light source within a store used to reinforce brand image; can also be a type of task lighting or accent light

Digital signage: digital displays that project messages on a screen using technologies like LCD and LED

Dwell time: the amount of time a customer spends looking at a display or in-store merchandise

Endless aisles: the concept that online shopping enables customers to shop a wide range of products as they are not tied to square footage

Experiential retail: shopping experience where brick-and-mortar customers participate in activities as a way to connect and engage with the brand and product offerings

Extended reality: also known as cross reality; includes virtual reality, augmented reality, and mixed reality

Facial recognition: technology that reads a digital image to identify a person (gender, age, etc.)

Forms: three-dimensional model of a torso or body originally used for sewing and draping

Freestanding fixtures: fixtures on wheels or bases that can be moved from one location to the next based on inventory level and store layout

Guideshop: used by e-commerce brands to provide a brick-and-mortar retail presence. A retail environment that allows customers to touch, feel and try on apparel and accessories before placing an order for the item; it is like a showroom.

Heat mapping: type of graph or data visualization technique that uses variation in color to show in-store foot traffic and patterns

Indoor location based services: a type of beacon technology that informs in-store shoppers of events, experiences, and product location in order to keep customers in the store

Informational signage: also referred to as departmental, directional, organization, or wayfinding signage; in-store signage used to inform and direct shoppers

Infrared sensors: motion-activated electronic sensors that trigger responses as a result of movement

Internet of Things (IoT): network of connected objects that collect and exchange data through technologies such as sensors and software programs

Machine learning: the process of computers collecting information based on observations and real-world interactions with its users in order to make product and service recommendations

Mannequin: human-like figure used to display apparel and accessories

Mass customization: the ability to personalize products while working within the constraints of mass production

Mixed reality: also known as hybrid reality; users are immersed in their existing environment as they also interact with a virtual environment

Mobile checkout: the ability to complete a purchase throughout the store via devices that are not anchored to a specific location in-store

Mobile commerce: m-commerce; the ability to buy and sell products and services through mobile devices using the internet

Multi-channel retail: shopping experience in which purchases can be made from different platforms, such as e-commerce site, catalog, or television

Multi-sensory experience: in-store experience that engages sound, sight, touch, smell, and taste in order to create an emotional connection with shoppers

Omnichannel retail: shopping experience where existing channels are integrated to provide a seamless shopping experience.

Outdoor location based services: a type of beacon technology that connects retailers with customers using geolocation services in order to draw customers into the store

Outdoor signage: also referred to as exterior signage; signage found outside a store that informs passersby what the store is all about

Persuasive signage: signage that advertises a promotion or product, often used to highlight new, seasonal, or sale merchandise

Phygital retail: shopping experience in which the brick-and-mortar (physical) environment and digital technologies interact with one another

Point of purchase items (POP): merchandise located in the area near the cash wrap; acts as suggestive selling or convenient add-on purchases

Push notifications: messages that appear as pop-ups on mobile devices for users who have installed corresponding apps

QR code: quick response code; type of two-dimensional bar code that is scanned (typically by a smartphone) and redirects the user to a website, advertisement, or other information

Realistic mannequins: type of mannequin that most closely resembles a human being

RFID: radio frequency identification; a tracking technology that allows retailers to access to real-time inventory updates

See now, buy now: movement in the retail industry where customers purchase product for immediate use rather than waiting months for production

Sensing technology: type of technology that utilizes sensors to detect, understand, and respond to movement or other activities in the physical retail environment.

Smart mannequin: mannequins that communicate with shoppers

Smart mirror: also known as smart display or digital mirror; two-way mirror with a display where shoppers can communicate with the retailer and/or sales associate

Social commerce: the purchasing of products and services through social media platforms

Square footage: measurement of area within a store; length $\times$ width

Standard fixtures: retail fixtures that are not manufactured and produced for a specific retailer and/or business but rather are available for general purchases

Store planning: the analysis, planning, and implementation of how retail stores strategically utilize the store's square footage to display merchandise

Task lighting: light sources that focus on specific areas of a store to help retailers and shoppers see better to accomplish a task

Transition area: also known as decompression zone; entrance of a retail store that introduces customers to the retail environment

User-generated content: content created by consumers and shared publicly about product or services, often as reviews via social media, videos, images, and blogs

Virtual mannequin: digital mannequins; mannequins that are visible through projection technology

Virtual reality: uses computer-generated simulations that create artificial digital environments that replace the real world

Visual merchandising: in-store displays and product placement used by retailers to show brand aesthetic and merchandise offerings in order to maximize sales

Wall-mounted fixtures: fixtures that are anchored to store walls, such as shelves and bracketed hang bars

Additional Resources

In addition to the brands, retailers, and companies you were introduced to in the text, here are some additional resources to explore:

Burberry Social Store: Burberryplc.com
Catchoom: catchoom.com
Dor: getdor.com
Facenote: facenote.me
FindMine: findmine.com
Genostyle: genostyle.com
MAC Cosmetics Innovation Lab
Mystore-E: mystore-e.com
Narvar: corp.narvar.com
Optoro: optoro.com
Rich Relevance: richrelevance.com
Slyce: slyce.it
Spacee: spacee.com
Starship Technologies: starship.xyz
SwiftGo: swiftgo.com
Trax Technology: traxretail.com
Volumental: volumental.com
Zappar: zappar.com

Companion Website Resources

Online resources to accompany this book are available at: www.bloomsburyonlineresources.com/swipe-scan-shop. Please type the URL into your web browser and follow the instructions to access the Companion Website. If you experience any problems, please contact Bloomsbury at: companionwebsites@bloomsbury.com

Works Cited

06/20/2017. "Report: This Is Why Consumers Shop in Stores." *RIS News*, June 20, 2017. https://risnews.com/report-why-consumers-shop-stores.

"2020 Facts & Figures // Instagram Statistics." Social Media Perth #SMPerth, May 22, 2020. https://www.smperth.com/resources/instagram/2020-instagram-statistics/.

"3D And Augmented Reality Product Visualization Platform." *Augment*. Accessed April 9, 2020. http://www.augment.com/blog/virtual-reality-vs-augmented-reality/.

Admin. "Levitating Floating Display." *Virtual On*. Accessed April 9, 2020. *https://virtualongroup.com/levitation-devicefloating-display/*.

"All WeChat Features in 2020." *QP Software*. Accessed May 27, 2020. https://qpsoftware.net/blog/all-wechat-features-2020.

Barry, Doug. "History of Mannequins Tracks the Aesthetic Tyranny of Consumerism." *Jezebel*. Jezebel, December 8, 2013. https://jezebel.com/history-of-mannequins-tracks-the-aesthetic-tyranny-of-c-1479024012.

Begum, Tahmina. "Zara Has Replaced Mannequins With Augmented Reality To Try To Change The Way We Shop." Huffingtonpost.co.uk, April, 17, 2018. https://www.huffingtonpost.co.uk/entry/zara-augmented-reality-mannequins_uk_5ad5bcf3e4b0edca2cbd9542?guccounter=1&guce_referrer=aHR0cHM6Ly93d3cuZ29vZ2xlLmNvbS8&guce_referrer_sig=AQAAAMH8YwNyH2qE_rBEPt-9V9XHyHeefrm0HbBDeL6HDBrfoWjyM6UcTsXrIb1bkPc13J3UtrPfFk0Uv3S6JNOSMISBQ1h0lCX0NdE6zE72_LpHWbezYjXDxtYaARs8aVcmnfeNf3hqrwa0vBiWPlLR_7wTB0SwXY2Zyrsw0QWz-xiT

Berthiaume, Dan. "Ulta Beauty Shoppers Behold New AR, AI Features." *Chain Store Age*. Accessed April 29, 2020. https://chainstoreage.com/technology/ulta-beauty-shoppers-behold-new-ar-ai-features.

Bettencourt, Jaime. "The Power of Experiential Retail Marketing." *Total Retail*, March 13, 2019. https://www.mytotalretail.com/article/the-power-of-experiential-retail-marketing/.

Bhattarai, Abha. "5 Ways the Future of Retail Is Already Here." chicagotribune.com. *Chicago Tribune*, May 13, 2019. https://www.chicagotribune.com/lifestyles/style/ct-future-retail-shopping-20180205-story.html.

Binlot, Ann. "Best Retail Experience Of 2018: Nike House Of Innovation 000." *Forbes*. *Forbes* Magazine, December 21, 2018. https://www.forbes.com/sites/abinlot/2018/12/21/best-retail-experience-of-2018-nike-house-of-innovation-000/#6d1c9d566597.

Bloem, Craig. "84 Percent of People Trust Online Reviews As Much As Friends. Here's How to Manage What They See." *Inc.com*. *Inc.*, July 31, 2017. https://www.inc.com/craig-bloem/84-percent-of-people-trust-online-reviews-as-much-.html.

Bloomberg.com. *Bloomberg*. Accessed April 9, 2020. https://www.bloomberg.com/news/articles/2017-03-20/apple-s-next-big-thing.

"Body Positivity in Fashion: From Fringe to Mainstream." *Highsnobiety*. June 1, 2017. https://www.highsnobiety.com/2017/05/21/body-positivity-in-fashion/.

Cammareri, Izzy. "Ordre." *ORDRE*, June 6, 2019. *https://www.ordre.com/en/news/what-5g-means-for-fashion-1218*.

"Can See-Now-Buy-Now Save Department Stores?" *Glossy*, May 29, 2018. https://www.glossy.co/fashion/department-stores-are-counting-on-the-success-of-see-now-buy-now.

Chamberlain, Lauryn. "Over 75 Percent Of Consumers Are Inspired To Make Purchases By Visual Content." GeoMarketing by Yext, October 27, 2017. https://geomarketing.com/over-75-percent-of-consumers-are-inspired-to-make-purchases-by-visual-content.

Cheng, Andria. "Why Amazon Go May Soon Change The Way We Shop." *Forbes*. *Forbes* Magazine, January 13, 2019. https://www.forbes.com/sites/andriacheng/2019/01/13/why-amazon-go-may-soon-change-the-way-we-want-to-shop/#5d048ee26709.

"CIBO Express Markets to Use Amazon Cashierless Tech." Visual Merchandising and Store Design. Accessed April 29, 2020. https://www.vmsd.com/content/cibo-express-markets-use-amazon-cashierless-tech?oly_enc_id=1784G5382467D2V).

Clement, J. "US Population with a Social Media Profile 2019." Statista, August 9, 2019. https://www.statista.com/statistics/273476/percentage-of-us-population-with-a-social-network-profile/.

"Clients & News." *Clients & News*. Accessed April 9, 2020. *http://www.retailsmart.com/clients-news*.

"Computer Vision." *ScienceDaily*. *ScienceDaily*. Accessed April 29, 2020. https://www.sciencedaily.com/terms/computer_vision.htm.

Coresight Research. "From Runway to Checkout: The See-Now-Buy-Now Trend in Fashion." *Coresight Research*, December 7, 2019. https://www.fung globalretailtech.com/research/runway-checkout -see-now-buy-now-trend-fashion/.

Danziger, Pamela N. "How A Design Firm Is Helping Target, Ulta And Best Buy Ditch Omnichannel For A New 'Harmonic' Model." *Forbes*. *Forbes* Magazine, May 2, 2019. https://www.forbes.com/sites /pamdanziger/2019/05/02/how-target-ulta-and -best-buy-abandoned-omnichannel-strategies -to-harmonize-customer-engagement /#3ce3eb7f523e.

Danziger, Pamela N. "Showfields Imagines A New Kind Of Department Store Combining Retail With Theater." *Forbes*. *Forbes* Magazine, September 19, 2019. https://www.forbes.com/sites/pamdanziger/ 2019/09/20/showfields-imagines-a-new-kind-of -department-store-combining-retail-with-theater /#3c2817166f1b.

"Demographics of Mobile Device Ownership and Adoption in the United States." Pew Research Center: Internet, Science & Tech. Pew Research Center. Accessed April 29, 2020. https://www .pewresearch.org/internet/fact-sheet/mobile/.

"Digital Signage: Full Solution Signage Provider - Scala." www.scala.com. Accessed April 29, 2020. https://www.scala.com/en/casestudies/#16679 category:retail.

DIRAdmin. "Shoppers Want to Be Left Alone in Stores: HRC Retail Advisory." *Digital Imaging Reporter*, May 10, 2018. https://direporter.com/industry-news /shoppers-want-left-alone-stores-hrc-retail-advisory.

DMI, Simon . "20 Influencer Marketing Statistics That Will Surprise You." Digital Marketing Institute. Digital Marketing Institute, November 15, 2019. https://digitalmarketinginstitute.com/en-us/blog/20 -influencer-marketing-statistics-that-will-surprise -you.

Dress Forms USA. "The Early History of Dress Forms and Mannequins." Dress Forms USA. Accessed April 9, 2020. *https://dressformsusa.com/blogs/posts/the -early-history-of-dress-forms-and-mannequins*.

Dress Forms USA. "Dress Forms – What Are They & How to Use Them." Dress Forms USA. Accessed May 4, 2020. https://dressformsusa.com/blogs/posts /dress-forms-what-are-they-how-to-use-them.

"Effective Use of Lighting in Retail Spaces." The four types of lighting that are used in retail setting. Accessed April 9, 2020. https://fluorescentman lighting.com/blog/Effective Use of Lighting in Retail Spaces/74.

"EuroShop TradeFairs." EuroShop. Accessed April 29, 2020. https://www.euroshop-tradefair.com/en /EuroShop_Trade_Fairs.

Faggella, Daniel. "What Is Machine Learning?" Emerj. Emerj, February 26, 2020. https://emerj.com /ai-glossary-terms/what-is-machine-learning/.

Frankel, Judy. "Shopping With An Avatar." *HuffPost*. *HuffPost*, February 20, 2017. https://www.huffpost .com/entry/shopping-with-an-avatar_b_58ab1b 93e4b0b0e1e0e20dfe?guccounter=1&guce_ referrer=aHR0cHM6Ly93d3cuZ29vZ2xlLmNvbS 8&guce_referrer_sig=AQAAAHD-lyCsqGxjM db1T8i-P2mrRf1-kbmrKMl_DArO4R1gxwVcJj3brSG hmlviOVmR2janNqjd0XT9iSlAft1wDL3ZmIrucfVI -qGbS4UqnryygC-VqFVGfpdZ3Cp1oiFDrLvuMC pntf3b_eqg6CtbXMkNhRJcRAC63wpvHH-eVkaQ.

"FutureProof Retail." FutureProof Retail. Accessed April 9, 2020. https://futureproofretail.com/.

Gesenhues, Amy. "Social Media Ad Spend to Surpass Print for First Time." Marketing Land, October 15, 2019. https://marketingland.com/social-media-ad -spend-to-surpass-print-for-first-time-268998.

Goode, Lauren. "Get Ready to Hear a Lot More About 'XR'." *Wired*. Conde Nast, January 7, 2019. https:// www.wired.com/story/what-is-xr/.

"Headworks 3D Holographic Mannequin." Headworks 3D Holographic Mannequin. Accessed April 9, 2020. http://www.headworks.co.uk/.

Helm, Joanne. "How to Sync In-Store Visual Merchandising With Your Marketing Strategy." iQmetrix. Accessed April 9, 2020. http://www .iqmetrix.com/blog/how-to-sync-in-store-visual -merchandising-with-your-marketing-strategy.

Hendriksz, Vivian. "Tommy Hilfiger Reveals New Runway Concept #TOMMYNOW." Fashionunited. Fashionunited, April 29, 2020. https://fashionunited .uk/news/fashion/tommy-hilfiger-reveals-new -runway-concept-tommynow/2016090721684.

Hermesauto. "US Retailers Install Cameras That Guess People's Shopping Habits." *The Straits Times*, April 28, 2019. https://www.straitstimes.com/world/united -states/us-retailers-install-cameras-that-guess -peoples-shopping-habits.

IA, Compliant. "5 Retail Merchandising Trends to Watch Out for in 2020." Retail Operations, March 3, 2020. https://blog.compliantia.com/2018/12/04 /5-retail-merchandising-trends-to-watch-out-for -in-2019/.

"IDummy Smart Mannequins." iDummy Smart Mannequin for Made to Measure and Garment *Design*. Accessed April 9, 2020. *http://www .yinusainc.com/main/idummy-smart-mannequin*.

Ingram, Bob, Progressive Grocer., and Progressive Grocer. "A Greener Bottom Line With Sustainable Store Lighting." Progressive Grocer. Accessed May 27, 2020. *https://progressivegrocer.com /greener-bottom-line-sustainable-store-lighting*.

"Inside Nike's Store of the Future." *Ad Age*, November 15, 2018. https://adage.com/article/digital/inside-nike-s-store-future/315633.

"In-Store, Atmosphere Counts. And Shoppers Say That Music Helps." Marketing Charts, September 19, 2018. https://www.marketingcharts.com/industries/retail-and-e-commerce-78248.

In-Store Virtual Dressing. Accessed April 29, 2020. https://www.trimirror.com/Solutions/InStore.

"Interactive Mirrors - The Future of Retail?" *Outform*, March 16, 2017. https://www.outform.com/interactive-mirrors-the-future-of-retail/.

John Lewis. Accessed April 29, 2020. https://www.johnlewispresscentre.com/image/details/119695.

Johnston, Lisa. "Amazon Just Walk Out Tech Now Available to Retailers." *RIS News*. Accessed April 9, 2020. https://risnews.com/amazon-just-walk-out-tech-now-available-retailers?utm_source=Push Engage&utm_medium=push&utm_campaign=PushEngage.

Judi. "The History Of Mannequins – from King Tut's Tomb to the 21st Century -." *Mannequin Madness* Blog, December 13, 2019. *https://blog.mannequinmadness.com/2010/07/mannequin-histor/*.

Khan, Humayun. "How Retailers Manipulate Sight, Smell, and Sound to Trigger Purchase Behavior in Consumers." *Shopify*, April 25, 2016. https://www.shopify.com/retail/119926083-how-retailers-manipulate-sight-smell-and-sound-to-trigger-purchase-behavior-in-consumers.

Kharpal, Arjun. "Everything You Need to Know about WeChat - China's Billion-User Messaging App." *CNBC*. CNBC, February 4, 2019. https://www.cnbc.com/2019/02/04/what-is-wechat-china-biggest-messaging-app.html.

Lockwood, Lisa. "Tommy Hilfiger to Stage Next 'See-Now-Buy-Now' Show in Paris." WWD. WWD, January 8, 2019. https://wwd.com/fashion-news/shows-reviews/tommy-hilfiger-to-stage-next-see-now-buy-now-show-in-paris-1202949325/.

Lutz, Ashley. "Nordstrom Could Start Using Pinterest To Make Merchandising Decisions." *Business Insider. Business Insider*, July 9, 2013. http://www.businessinsider.com/how-nordstrom-is-using-pinterest-2013-7.

"Macy's 'American Icons' Campaign Returns This Spring." Macy's, Inc., April 16, 2014. *https://www.macysinc.com/news-media/press-releases/detail/480/macys-american-icons-campaign-returns-this-spring*.

Maltseva, Diana. "The Future of Retail: How IoT Is Transforming the Retail Industry." ClickZ, September 30, 2019. *https://www.clickz.com/the-future-of-retail-how-iot-is-transforming-the-retail-industry/214543/*.

Matchar, Emily. "This Morphing Mannequin Could Transform the Fashion Industry." Smithsonian.com. Smithsonian Institution, February 29, 2016. https://www.smithsonianmag.com/innovation/this-morphing-mannequin-could-transform-fashion-industry-180958240/.

Merle, Leo. "Using NFC Tags in Brick and Mortar Stores." ZineOne, November 13, 2019. https://www.zineone.com/blogdetails/using-nfc-tags-in-brick-and-mortar-stores/.

Milnes, Hilary. "Can see-now-buy-now save department stores?" *Glossy*, January 18, 2018. Glossy.co/fashion-calendar/department-stores-are-counting-on-the-success-of-see-now-buy-now.

Mitchell, Josh, and Sarah Chaney. "US Retail Sales Jumped 0.6% in July." The Wall Street Journal. Dow Jones & Company, August 15, 2017. https://www.wsj.com/articles/u-s-retail-sales-jumped-0-6-in-july-1502800549.

Moltin. "In-Store Mobile Self Checkout." *Moltin*. Accessed April 9, 2020. https://www.moltin.com/commerce-solutions/mobile-self-checkout/.

Morris, Leighann. "The Complete History of Mannequins: Garbos, Twiggies, Barbies and Beyond." Hopes&Fears, November 20, 2015. http://www.hopesandfears.com/hopes/city/fashion/213389-history-of-mannequins.

"Multi-Sensory Design for Retail – How to Make the Most of All Five Senses." Visual Merchandising and Store Design. Accessed April 9, 2020. http://www.vmsd.com/content/multi-sensory-design-retail-how-make-most-all-five-senses.

"Nordstrom Wants Brands to Embrace the 'Size Spectrum'." *Digiday*, May 20, 2018. *https://digiday.com/marketing/nordstrom-wants-brands-embrace-size-spectrum/*.

Oatman-Stanford, Hunter. "Retail Therapy: What Mannequins Say About Us." *Collectors Weekly*. Accessed May 5, 2020. https://www.collectorsweekly.com/articles/what-mannequins-say-about-us/.

Ollila, Erin. "4 Brands That Mastered the Omnichannel Customer Experience." SmarterCX, February 28, 2019. *https://smartercx.com/4-brands-that-mastered-the-omnichannel-customer-experience/*.

Orndorff, Brandon. "Release - The State of Brick & Mortar 2017." Mood Media, February 17, 2020. https://us.moodmedia.com/featured-news/state-brick-mortar-2017/.

Orvis, Guinevere. "The Ultimate Guide to Retail Store Layouts." *Shopify*, January 18, 2017. https://www.shopify.com/retail/the-ultimate-guide-to-retail-store-layouts.

Petro, Greg. "How 'See-Now-Buy-Now' Is Rewiring Retail." *Forbes. Forbes* Magazine, May 22, 2018.

https://www.forbes.com/sites/gregpetro/2018/01/31/how-see-now-buy-now-is-rewiring-retail/.

Pierce, David. "The Curious Comeback of the Dreaded QR Code." *Wired*. Conde Nast. Accessed April 9, 2020. https://www.wired.com/story/the-curious-comeback-of-the-dreaded-qr-code/.

Pymnts. "How Kohl's Is Moving Toward Millennial Shoppers." PYMNTS.com. PYMNTS 60 60 PYMNTS.com, December 6, 2018. https://www.pymnts.com/news/retail/2018/how-kohls-it-thinking-differently-as-it-moves-on-millennial-shoppers/.

Quora. "The Difference Between Virtual Reality, Augmented Reality And Mixed Reality." *Forbes*. *Forbes* Magazine, February 2, 2018. https://www.forbes.com/sites/quora/2018/02/02/the-difference-between-virtual-reality-augmented-reality-and-mixed-reality/#2d90c80c2d07.

"Rebecca Minkoff Tosses Cash Registers with New Connected Store." *Latest News*. Accessed April 9, 2020. https://www.retaildive.com/ex/mobilecommercedaily/rebecca-minkoff-tosses-cash-registers-with-new-soho-connected-store.

"Report: The State of Consumer Behavior 2020 - Raydiant: Your Digital Signage Company." *Raydiant*, January 28, 2020. https://www.raydiant.com/blog/report-the-state-of-consumer-behavior-2020/.

Retail Design Blog. "BucketFeet Soho Pop-up Shop, New York City." *Retail Design Blog*. Accessed April 9, 2020. https://retaildesignblog.net/2014/07/04/bucketfeet-soho-pop-up-shop-new-york-city/.

"Retail Marketing Lift-And-Learn Digital Signage, Kiosks, and In-Store Analytics Software." *Perch*. Accessed April 9, 2020. https://www.perchinteractive.com/.

"Retail Store Layout Design and Planning." Smartsheet. Accessed April 29, 2020. https://www.smartsheet.com/store-layout.

"Retail's Secret Weapon: High-Tech Heat Maps." *CNNMoney*. Cable News Network. Accessed April 9, 2020. https://money.cnn.com/2016/08/29/technology/prism-technology-shopping/index.html.

Reuters. "Amazon to Sell Cashierless Technology to Retailers." *The Business of Fashion*. The Business of Fashion, March 9, 2020. https://www.businessoffashion.com/articles/news-analysis/amazon-to-sell-cashierless-technology-to-retailers?utm_source=daily-digest-newsletter&utm_campaign=1660686893329897&utm_term=11&utm_medium=email.

Reyhle, Nicole. "Engaging All 5 Senses of Your Customers." Retail Minded, September 21, 2012. https://retailminded.com/engaging-5-senses-customers/.

"RFID in Retail: RFID Software." RIOT Insight. Accessed April 29, 2020. https://www.riotinsight.com/article-rfid-in-retail.

Sammynickalls. "Lush Is Using Machine Learning and AI to Make Wasteful Packaging and Signage Irrelevant." Adweek. Adweek, March 13, 2019. https://www.adweek.com/brand-marketing/lush-is-using-machine-learning-and-ai-to-make-wasteful-packaging-and-signage-irrelevant/.

Scheithauer, Glenn. "The Art & Science of Experiential Retailing." RIS News. Accessed April 29, 2020. https://risnews.com/art-science-experiential-retailing?utm_source=PushEngage&utm_medium=push&utm_campaign=PushEngage.

Schulte, Liz. "Beacons in Retail: What You Need to Know." Beacons in Retail: What You Need to Know. Accessed April 9, 2020. https://foreword.mbsbooks.com/beacons-in-retail-what-you-need-to-know#gsc.tab=0.

Segran, Elizabeth. "Rebecca Minkoff Took 'See Now, Buy Now' to a Whole New Level This Year." *Fast Company*. *Fast Company*, September 12, 2016. https://www.fastcompany.com/4018896/rebecca-minkoff-took-see-now-buy-now-to-a-whole-new-level-this-year.

Segran, Elizabeth. "Is Fashion Week Irrelevant? Rebecca Minkoff And Anna Sui Weigh In." *Fast Company*. *Fast Company*, September 7, 2017. https://www.fastcompany.com/40461496/is-fashion-week-dead-rebecca-minkoff-and-anna-sui-debate.

"Sephora Blends Mobile with Bricks-and-Mortar for First Connected Boutique." *Latest News*. Accessed April 9, 2020. *https://www.retaildive.com/ex/mobilecommercedaily/sephora-blends-mobile-with-bricks-and-mortar-for-first-connected-boutique-experience*.

"Sephora Muscles into Subscription Services with Help from Mobile Offers." *Latest News*. Accessed May 5, 2020. https://www.retaildive.com/ex/mobilecommercedaily/sephora-forays-into-subscription-service-with-help-from-mobile-offers.

"Sephora Redefines Shopping for Loyalists with Unique Mobile App." *Latest News*. Accessed April 29, 2020. https://www.retaildive.com/ex/mobilecommercedaily/sephora-redefines-shopping-for-loyalists-with-unique-mobile-app.

Silva, Michelle da. "Proximity Marketing: How to Attract More Shoppers With Beacon Technology." *Shopify*, April 12, 2017. *https://www.shopify.com/retail/the-ultimate-guide-to-using-beacon-technology-for-retail-stores*.

Simpson, Jeff. "Deloitte Study: Digital Influence Redefines the Customer Experience - Press Release: Deloitte US." Deloitte United States, July 12, 2017. https://www2.deloitte.com/us/en/pages/about-deloitte/articles/press-releases/deloitte-study-digital-influence-redefines-customer-experience.html.

Skrovan, Sandy. "How Shoppers Use Their Smartphones in Stores." *Retail Dive*, June 7, 2017. https://www.retaildive.com/news/how-shoppers-use-their-smartphones-in-stores/444147/.

Smith, Ray A. "Mannequins Make a Comeback." *The Wall Street Journal*. Dow Jones & Company, April 9, 2014. https://www.wsj.com/articles/mannequins-make-a-comeback-1396996329.

Spectrio. "Seven Ways Overhead Music Affects the Shopping Experience." *Spectrio* Blog. Accessed April 29, 2020. https://blogs.spectrio.com/seven-ways-overhead-music-affects-the-shopping-experience.

Sterling, Greg. "Mobile Now Accounts for Nearly 70% of Digital Media Time [ComScore]." *Marketing Land*, March 29, 2017. https://marketingland.com/mobile-now-accounts-nearly-70-digital-media-time-comscore-210094.

"Stories: Q&A: Jean Marc Mesguich, Founder of Window Mannequins." sportswear. Accessed May 5, 2020. https://www.sportswear-international.com/news/stories/QA-Jean-Marc-Mesguich-founder-of-Window-Mannequins-10318.

Strange, Adario. "Forget Augmented Reality Glasses-AR Windows Are Here Today." *Mashable. Mashable*, May 23, 2017. *http://mashable.com/2017/05/23/augmented-reality-window/#wc0wuuutwqq0.*

Studionorth, and Name *. "What's next in Retail? At NRF17, the Answer Was Data, Data, Data." *StudioNorth*, April 26, 2018. https://www.studionorth.com/whats-next-retail-nrf17-answer-data-data-data/.

"The Company Making Mannequins Molded On Disabled People." *GirlTalkHQ*, October 2, 2016. https://girltalkhq.com/company-making-mannequins-molded-disabled-people/.

"The North Face Opens SoHo Concept Store." Visual Merchandising and Store Design. Accessed April 9, 2020. *https://www.vmsd.com/content/north-face-opens-soho-concept-store?oly_enc_id=1784G5382467D2V.*

theretailintelligence.com Is For Sale. Accessed May 5, 2020. http://www.theretailintelligence.com/mixing-physical-digital-phygital/.

"The Rise of Technology in Experiential Retail." www.retailcustomerexperience.com, August 6, 2019. https://www.retailcustomerexperience.com/blogs/the-rise-of-technology-in-experiential-retail/?utm_source=RCE&utm_medium=email&utm_campaign=EMNA&utm_content=2019-08-06.

"Three Seasons in, See-Now-Buy-Now Is Going Nowhere." *Digiday*, September 18, 2017. https://digiday.com/marketing/three-seasons-see-now-buy-now-going-nowhere/.

TodayShow. "Nike Introduces Mannequins of All Shapes, Sizes and Abilities in New Store." TODAY.com, June 6, 2019. https://www.today.com/series/love-your-body/nike-introduces-mannequins-all-shapes-sizes-abilities-new-store-t155706.

"V&A · Introducing Mary Quant." Victoria and Albert Museum. Accessed April 9, 2020. *https://www.vam.ac.uk/articles/introducing-mary-quant.*

"VR, AR, MR, XR – What Are All These?" *Valmet*. Accessed April 29, 2020. https://www.valmet.com/media/articles/all-articles/vr-ar-mr-xr-what-are-all-these/.

Wahba, Phil. "Target CEO: 'We Realized We Were Making Customers Work Too Hard." *Fortune. Fortune*, November 9, 2015. http://fortune.com/2015/10/27/target-merchandising/.

Wahba, Phil. "Abercrombie & Fitch Bets On Cool Fitting Rooms to Revive Brand." *Fortune. Fortune*, August 25, 2017. *https://fortune.com/2017/08/25/abercrombie-fitch-fitting-room/.*

"What Is Computer Vision? - Definition from Techopedia." Techopedia.com. Accessed April 29, 2020. https://www.techopedia.com/definition/32309/computer-vision.

Williams, Robert. "Macy's Back-to-School Push Debuts with Snapchat Shopping, TikTok Challenge." Mobile Marketer, August 6, 2019. https://www.mobilemarketer.com/news/macys-back-to-school-push-debuts-with-snapchat-shopping-tiktok-challenge/560292/.

www.fibre2fashion.com. "H&M To Accelerate Transformation on Digitalisation." Fibre2Fashion. Accessed April 9, 2020. *https://www.fibre2fashion.com/news/company-news/apparel-news/h-m-to-accelerate-transformation-on-digitalisation-246860-newsdetails.htm.*

Photo Credits

Thank you for the talented creatives who shared samples of their work to bring retail examples to life.

And a shout-out to Cody Banks for his graphic design work!

Kiyoshi Ota/Bloomberg via Getty Images (Image 0.1); Creative Commons stockmanngroup (Image 1.1); Budrul Chukrut/SOPA Images/LightRocket via Getty Images (Image 1.2); K. Schaefer (Image 1.3); Spencer Platt/Getty Images (Image 1.4); K. Schaefer (Image 1.5); WindowsWear (Image 1.6); Cristina Arias for Getty Images (Image 1.7); K. Schaefer (Image 1.8); Mark Mainz/Getty Images (Image 1.9); Mark Kauzlarich/Bloomberg (Image 1.10); Sue Hawks (Image 1.11); K. Schaefer (Image 1.12); Eugene Gologursky/Getty Images (Image 1.13); K. Schaefer (Image 1.14); Tomohiro Ohsumi/Bloomberg via Getty Images (Image 1.15); Jeffrey Greenberg/Universal Images Group via Getty Images (Image 1.16); View Pictures/Universal Images Group via Getty Images (Image 1.17); WindowsWear (Image 1.18); K. Schaefer (Image 1.19); javitrapero/iStock and Getty Images (Image 1.20); Getty Images Stock Photo (Image 1.21); Marvin Woodyatt/WireImage, Getty Images (Image 1.22); K. Schaefer (Image 1.23-24); Demetrius Freeman/Bloomberg via Getty Images (Image 1.25); Craig Winslow (Image 1.26-30); Jeenah Moon/Bloomberg via Getty Images (Image 2.1); Hulton Archive/Getty Images (Image 2.2); Apic/Getty Images (Image 2.3); Cyril Maitland/Mirrorpix/Getty Images (Image 2.4); JP Yim/Getty Images (Image 2.5); Chris McGrath/Getty Images (Image 2.6); Timothy Hiatt/Getty Images for Pottery Barn (Image 2.7); K. Schaefer (Image 2.8-15); Visual China Group via Getty Image (Image 2.16); Rachel Murray/Getty Images for Rebecca Minkoff (Image 2.17-18); Jaap Arriens/Nur Photo via Getty Images (Image 3.1); Luke MacGregor/Bloomberg via Getty Images (Image 3.2); K. Schaefer (Image 3.3-4); Lisa Lake/Getty Images (Image 3.5); Luke Sharrett/Bloomberg via Getty Images (Image 3.6); WindowsWear (Image 3.7); K. Schaefer (Image 3.8); Robert Alexander/Getty Images (Image 3.9); Cindy Ord/Getty Images for Uniqlo and Lemaire (Image 3.10); K. Schaefer (Image 3.11-13); Nicky Loh/Bloomberg via Getty Images (Image 3.14); Jonathan Wiggs/The Boston Globe via Getty Images (Image 3.15); K. Schaefer (Image 3.16-19); Cody Banks (Figure 3.20); Nicky Loh/Bloomberg via Getty Images (Image 3.21); Haniff Brown (Image 3.22-24); YOSHIKAZU TSUNO/AFT/Getty images (Image 4.1); Pablo Blazquez Dominguez/Getty Images (Image 4.2); View Pictures/Universal Images Group via Getty Images (Image 4.3); Sue Hawks (Image 4.4); Ed Reeve/View Pictures/Universal Images Group via Getty Images (Image 4.5); Koichi Kamoshida/Bloomberg via Getty Images (Image 4.6); Harbor Retail™ (Image 4.7); Ulrich Baumgarten via Getty Images (Image 4.8); Bernard Weil/Toronto Star via Getty Images (Image 4.9); K. Schaefer (Image 4.10-11); Visual Retailing (Image 4.11-13); View Pictures/Universal Images Group via Getty Images (Image 5.1); Jeff Schear/Getty Images for Under Armour (Image 5.2); "Apple Store" by bfishadow is licensed under CC BY 2.0. Photo credit: Creative Commons bfishadow (Image 5.3); K. Schaefer (Image 5.4); John Lewis Press Centre (Image 5.5); K. Schaefer (Image 5.6); MediaNews Group/Bay Area News via Getty Images (Image 5.7); "Lucky Brand Jeans" by JeepersMedia is licensed under CC BY 2.0. Photo credit: Creative Commons Jeepers Media (Image 5.8); Photo credit: J. Schear/Getty Images (Image 5.9); K. Schaefer (Image 5.10-12); Isa Foltin/Getty Images for Espirit (Image 5.13); WindowsWear (Image 5.14); K. Schaefer (Image 5.15-17), K. Schaefer (Image 6.1-2); Simon Dawson/Bloomberg

Index